South Africa

one of the world's great tourist destinations

South Africa offers an extraordinary variety of leisure options: game reserves, cosmopolitan cities, mountain resorts and pristine beaches. Lions and diamonds, ancient forts and tribal dancing, flickering campfire, the fish eagle's haunting cry . . .

Daytime diversions include coach tours, cruises, museums, art galleries and an extensive range of sporting opportunities. Night life encompasses the cocktail/cabaret/restaurant circuit, film festivals and the classical performing arts.

The scenery is magnificent, the climate sunny and mild, and the country's friendly hospitality is legendary. Accommodation standards are high, and wherever you go, you're sure of a warm welcome, comfort, good service, excellent food and fine wines.

Whether you want to relax and soak up the sunshine, enjoy the social whirl or follow a quest for adventure, South Africa has everything you're looking for - and more.

In its landscapes, people, wildlife and quality tourist infrastructure, South Africa has no equal on the continent. What's more, in your currency, the country offers an exceptional holiday bargain.

Many visitors return over and again to familiar resorts. Exciting discoveries await those who stray from the beaten track.

Happy travelling!

Although all possible care has been taken in researching, compiling, writing and editing the information provided in the contents of this travel guide, Satour cannot accept responsibility for any errors and/or omissions.

Contents

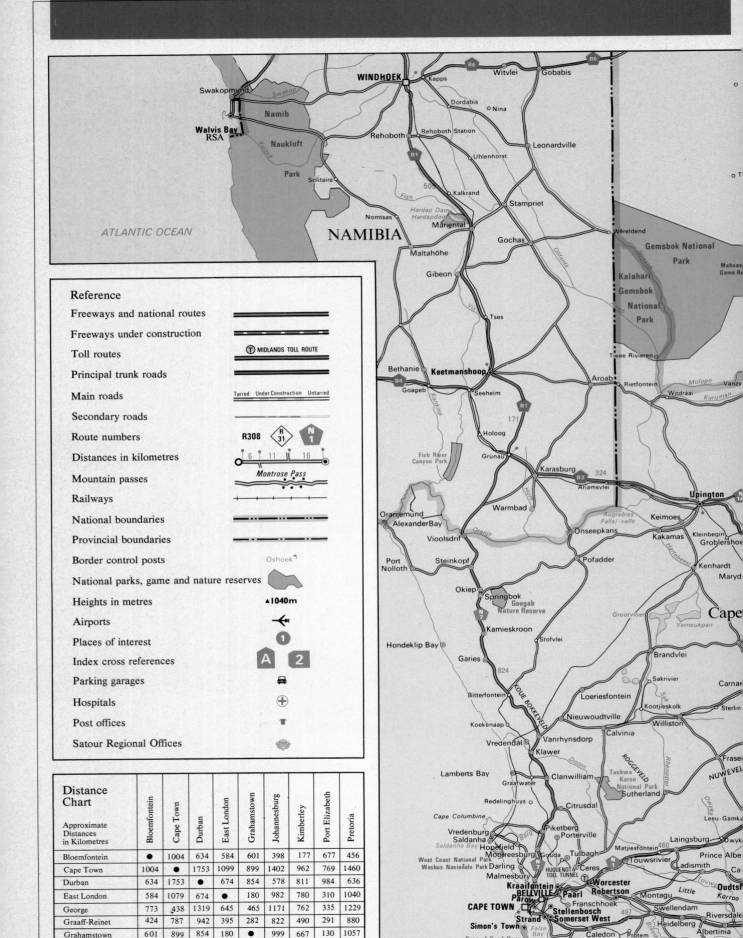

Reference

Freeways and national routes	
Freeways under construction	
Toll routes	ⓣ MIDLANDS TOLL ROUTE
Principal trunk roads	
Main roads	Tarred Under Construction Untarred
Secondary roads	
Route numbers	R308 〈R 31〉 N1
Distances in kilometres	6 11 16
Mountain passes	Montrose Pass
Railways	
National boundaries	
Provincial boundaries	
Border control posts	Oshoek
National parks, game and nature reserves	
Heights in metres	▲1040m
Airports	✈
Places of interest	①
Index cross references	A 2
Parking garages	🚗
Hospitals	✚
Post offices	⊤
Satour Regional Offices	

Distance Chart

Approximate Distances in Kilometres

	Bloemfontein	Cape Town	Durban	East London	Grahamstown	Johannesburg	Kimberley	Port Elizabeth	Pretoria
Bloemfontein	●	1004	634	584	601	398	177	677	456
Cape Town	1004	●	1753	1099	899	1402	962	769	1460
Durban	634	1753	●	674	854	578	811	984	636
East London	584	1079	674	●	180	982	780	310	1040
George	773	438	1319	645	465	1171	762	335	1229
Graaff-Reinet	424	787	942	395	282	822	490	291	880
Grahamstown	601	899	854	180	●	999	667	130	1057
Harrismith	328	1331	306	822	929	274	505	1068	332
Johannesburg	398	1402	578	982	999	●	472	1075	58
Kimberley	177	962	811	780	667	472	●	743	530

Copyright © Map Studio

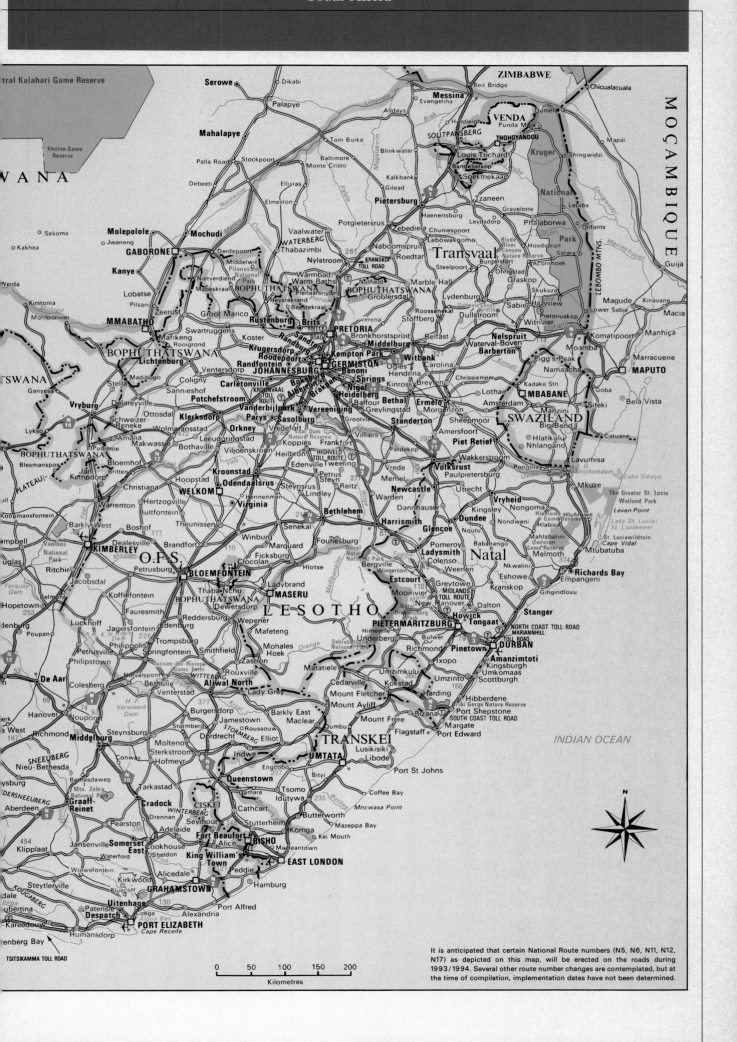

It is anticipated that certain National Route numbers (N5, N6, N11, N12, N17) as depicted on this map, will be erected on the roads during 1993/1994. Several other route number changes are contemplated, but at the time of compilation, implementation dates have not been determined.

0   50   100   150   200
Kilometres

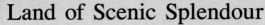

Land of Scenic Splendour

Few countries rival South Africa's scenic splendour. Rolling farmlands and fertile vineyards abound, traditional tribal villages, 20th century skylines . . .

It's easy to fall in love with the beauty of the south-western Cape and the Garden Route. Blessed with everything that is most impressive in nature, the region encompasses spectacular mountains, a prodigious floral kingdom, fishing harbours, broad white beaches and a sapphire sea. Dominating the northern end of the Cape Peninsula, Table Mountain, draped with its famous 'tablecloth', is renowned throughout the world.

Tranquil beaches and lagoons, rocky shores and charming seaside resorts dot the coastline from Mozambique to the mouth of the Orange River.

The interior also has its share of contrasts. In the Great Karoo's Valley of Desolation, giant dolerite pillars have been eroded into extraordinary shapes, and piles of boulders tower above the valley in a grand display of nature's sculpture. Namaqualand in spring has a splendour all of its own when the drab semi-desert is transformed into a blaze of brilliant blooms - from one horizon to another.

The Blyde River Canyon in the eastern Transvaal ranks as one of the scenic wonders of Africa. Winding along the floor of the canyon, the river is flanked by towering buttresses and cliffs in striking shades of yellow and red.

On Natal's western boundary, the craggy Drakensberg Mountains are an unforgettable sight in every season, while the midlands present a gentle, pastoral picture.

Pride and joy of the Orange Free State, the imposing golden cliffs of the north-eastern highlands rate high among the country's great natural assets.

Above left: Howick Falls, in the Umgeni Valley Nature Reserve — a popular spot among picnickers.

Right: One of the most photographed views in the world: Table Mountain taken from Bloubergstrand.

Left: Dominating the surroundings, the weathered sandstone Maltese Cross is one of many sculpted rock formations in the Cedarberg.

Left: *Pastoral landscape near Ermelo on the Transvaal highveld.*

Right: *In the Valley of Desolation at Graaff-Reinet, giant dolerite pillars have been eroded into extraordinary shapes.*

Below left: *The tranquil seaside resort of Wilderness lies on the Garden Route.*

Below: *Namaqualand in spring has a splendour all of its own.*

Above: *The craggy Drakensberg Mountains — an unforgettable sight all year round.*

Above right: *The Blyde River Canyon ranks among the scenic wonders of Africa.*

Right: *Sandstone cliffs guard the entrance to the Golden Gate National Park.*

A World in one Country

Since Jan van Riebeeck's time, South Africa has attracted settlers from the corners of the globe. Today, the country's cultural diversity is one of its most dynamic components.

Take a stroll down a busy city street and you're sure to encounter the briefcase brigade, socialites flaunting couturier chic, decorously cloaked Islamic matrons, beaded, blanketed Zulus, and students of every hue in regulation faded jeans.

Cathedral bells and the roar of traffic vie for attention, and in the shade of soaring superstructures, apartment blocks and synagogues rub shoulders with Victorian bungalows. Gracious Cape Dutch buildings recall the leisurely charm of vanished eras and the origins of the earliest settlers. And in far-flung rural areas, tribal people inhabit beehive huts, tilling the soil and herding cattle, ever mindful of the ancestral spirits.

South Africa's musical repertoire encompasses the traditions of the past and the most up-to-date dynamics of today: African drumbeat, ancient Indian rhythms, Afrikaans folk songs, Western classics, electronic pop and rock.

And the country's rich multicultural mix is strikingly reflected on its restaurant menus. Traditional Cape Malay dishes, Natal's spicy Indian heritage, pizza/pasta parlours, and French, Portuguese, Greek, German, Chinese and Japanese eateries.

Visitors looking for deeper insight into this fascinating cultural mosaic need only switch on the TV. The South African television network transmits programmes every day in English, Afrikaans and five Black languages. And on Sunday mornings, an Indian programme is presented in English, Tamil, Hindi and Gujerati!

Above: *Johannesburg is renowned for its opulent shopping centres.*

Below: *Cape minstrels sing Afrikaans folk songs with engaging vitality.*

Top and above: *Up-market hotels are found throughout the country.*

Below: *Options for sportsmen (and women) cover a wide spectrum, ranging from table tennis to hot air ballooning and yachting.*

6

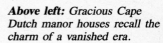

Above left: *Gracious Cape Dutch manor houses recall the charm of a vanished era.*

Above: *Oriental festivals add an exotic touch to the country's cultural diversity.*

Left: *In the rural areas, Zulus follow an ancient, traditional lifestyle.*

Right: *Exciting developments are taking place on the local musical circuits.*

Above left: *In Xhosa tribal society, married women wear elaborate turbans.*

Above: *South Africa's restaurants cater for a cosmopolitan clientele.*

Left: *A popular gathering place on Cape Town's Greenmarket Square.*

7

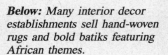

Good Buys

In the cities, you can buy anything from a karakul coat to a crocodile bag, antiques, handwoven rugs and individually designed treasures in gold, diamonds and other precious stones. Most visitors opt for exclusive jewellery, quality leather goods and haute couture.

Shopping for clothes is always in style, and at dozens of trendy boutiques, there's not a hint of anything remotely mass-produced. Quality and flair come with the designer labels.

Up-market interior decor establishments are blazing new trails with Africa-inspired accessories: bold batiks, artistic ceramics, candelabra and vividly painted sculptures. The panache is elegant enough to enhance the most tastefully decorated home.

Craftsmen practise ancient, intricate skills in aromatic Indian bazaars, and that's where you'll find filigree jewellery, oriental ornaments, silk saris and spices.

Curio shops and flea markets are the places to peruse for African arts, crafts and ethnic chic. Antique shops offer Cape Dutch, Victorian and Georgian furniture, rare books, old jewellery, maps and bric-a-brac.

For visitors to South Africa, shopping comes with a modest price tag. The current Rand value leans so heavily in your favour that your extravagances won't even begin to bend your travel allowance!

Above: *Intricate Venda beadwork is sold at roadside stalls and curio shops.*

Right: *Some shoppers opt for more expensive souvenirs.*

Below: *Many interior decor establishments sell hand-woven rugs and bold batiks featuring African themes.*

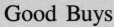

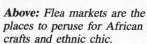

Above: *Flea markets are the places to peruse for African crafts and ethnic chic.*

Left: *Browsing for Christmas presents brings throngs to the major shopping centres.*

Right: *Manufacturing jewellers create treasures in gold, diamonds and other precious stones.*

8

Above: *Shells: the perfect gift for those who enjoy the simple things in life.*

Right: *For convenience, there's nothing to beat one-stop shopping under one roof.*

Right: *A bit of music is guaranteed to liven up the serious business of trading in the marketplace.*

Below: *Specialist boutiques cater for discriminating shoppers with five-star tastes.*

Below right: *Art in the park exhibitions are held throughout the country.*

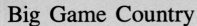

Big Game Country

In habitats from desert dunelands to savannah lands and shady subtropical forests, South Africa's game reserves are inhabited by an unparalleled variety of animal and bird species.

Major scene-stealers are probably the elephant, lion, leopard, buffalo and rhino (the 'Big Five'), but some visitors get just as much of a kick out of spotting a kudu, a comical warthog or a tiny pygmy shrew.

The lush vegetation of summer provides a camouflage for many species of game, but in winter (May to August), the grass is short and the animals are easily spotted. This is an ideal time to visit the reserves. Game-viewing is best in the early morning and late afternoon, and even on a quiet day, you're sure to see large numbers and varieties of game. Some species react nervously to the presence of people. Others pose obligingly for the camera.

At many parks, conducted game trails feature on the agenda. This is the finest way of getting close to nature. Some reserves offer four-wheel drive vehicles and the services of experienced rangers. Familiar with the foibles of the innumerable inhabitants of the bush, they're only too happy to share their anecdotes with you.

Provincial and National Parks encompass basic, self-catering establishments and top-of the-range accommodation. Luxurious, privately owned game lodges (mainly in the eastern Transvaal and northern Natal) usually provide off-the-beaten-track game drives and spotlight evening game-viewing excursions.

Whether you choose to rough it or join the jet set on safari, an incomparable experience awaits you in the South African wilderness.

Above: *In giraffe society, necking takes on extended dimensions . . .*

Below: *In the zebra community, stripes are always in style.*

Above: *Members of an elephant herd follow the matriarch to seek food, water or a shady resting place.*

Left: *Beware of the buffalo! His bovine appearance belies an unpredictable nature.*

Right: *The solitary leopard likes to spend his days napping in a tree.*

Left: Sometimes, romantic overtures seem very threatening!

Right: Largely nocturnal, the stately kudu seeks shade when the sun is high.

Far right: The broad, square muzzle of the white rhino is designed for grazing.

Above: No other creature in Africa is quite as imposing or regal as the elephant.

Below: The crowned eagle inhabits dense riverine forest.

Left: An up-market game lodge near the Kruger National Park.

11

Transvaal

A landlocked province, and the most northerly in South Africa, the Transvaal is bounded by the Cape Province, Botswana, Zimbabwe, Mozambique, Swaziland, Natal and the Orange Free State. The province has great beauty, immense mineral wealth and vast agricultural lands.

Much of the eastern Transvaal is subtropical lowveld, an area of rolling farmlands, woodland and savannah, famous internationally for the presence of some of the country's best game reserves. They offer exceptional opportunities for viewing large numbers and varieties of game.

The northern Transvaal and parts of the west are characterised by open plains, tall mountains and indigenous forests. A grassy plateau known as the highveld comprises most of the central and south-western Transvaal. Situated on the southern highveld plateau, the Witwatersrand is South Africa's most highly industrialised complex.

The Vaal River, principal tributary of the Orange River, forms the boundary between the Transvaal and the Orange Free State. The Vaal Dam provides water for the urban, industrial and mining complex of the Witwatersrand, Pretoria and Vereeniging; it's also a popular recreational drawcard, attracting large numbers of water sports enthusiasts. On some of the islands which divide the river into branches, holiday resorts have been developed.

Good roads, a healthy, invigorating climate and charming accommodation establishments will enhance your enjoyment of this wonderful region.

Witwatersrand and Environs

One hundred and sixty years ago, the area now known as the Witwatersrand was populated only by scattered (often warlike) tribes. Although the Boers who trekked from the Cape to the highveld in the 1830s must have been aware of the potential for conflict, they saw the advantages of good grazing and a deep and fertile soil. They settled in small, isolated groups, raised families, tended cattle and planted crops.

In 1886, an Australian prospector, George Harrison, stumbled upon the world's richest deposit of gold on a patch of windswept veld. Prospectors, speculators and adventurers arrived in the area from the four corners of the earth, and the pastoral landscape changed almost overnight.

Gold rush towns of shacks, saloons and brawls were rapidly transformed into modern concrete cities graced with parks and man-made lakes. To support the mining industry, roads and railways were built, agricultural production was greatly increased and manufacturing industries were developed.

At the hub of it all, Johannesburg grew around the mines and became the 'Gold Capital of the World'. And the country was catapulted into an economic boom.

Today, Johannesburg, Pretoria and the 'Vaal Triangle' towns of Vereeniging and Vanderbijlpark comprise the industrial and commercial heart of South Africa. To the east and west, towns merge one into the other in a great and growing concrete sprawl.

But much of the region has escaped the spread of industrial development; there are dozens of quiet retreats, country hotels and leisure resorts where city-dwellers can relax in an environment free of urban distractions.

Above: *The blue crane, South Africa's national bird, is protected in sanctuaries throughout the country.*

Above: *Starting the day in style at a popular Johannesburg hotel.*

Below: *Thrills and chills at the Rand Show, an international event held in Johannesburg during the Easter holidays every year.*

Below: *A perfect way to end the day: sundowners at sunset on the Hartbeespoort Dam.*

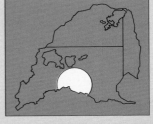

Above: *Shopping is always a pleasure at Plaza Square in Springs.*

Left: *Wild waves and raging rapids at Boksburg's inland 'seaside' resort.*

Right: *A handsome inhabitant of the De Wildt Cheetah Research Centre, west of Pretoria.*

Below: *Preparing for take-off: air show, Wonderboom Airport.*

Above: *A hot air balloon provides the finest views of the highveld farmlands.*

Places of Interest

C1 1 Austin Roberts Bird Sanctuary The park, named after an authority on South African birds and author of the first editions of what is now called 'Roberts' Birds of Southern Africa', offers sanctuary to water birds, blue crane, crowned crane, sacred ibis, heron and a rare black swan.

C3 2 Bezuidenhout Park The farm dates from the gold rush days and still boasts the original farmstead. Other facilities include a recreation centre, pool, restaurant and sports grounds.

C3 3 Boksburg An industrial and gold mining town. **Boksburg Lake** has good sailing and recreational facilities.

D1 4 Cullinan Tours are offered of the world-renowned volcanic pipe diamond mine where the 3,106-carat Cullinan diamond was found.

B3 5 Delta Park The headquarters of the Wildlife Society of South Africa incorporates a modern conservation centre and the **Florence Bloom Bird Sanctuary.**

B1 6 De Wildt Cheetah Research Centre On Saturdays group tours of this well-known breeding centre for cheetah, king cheetah, wild dog and brown hyena are available.

C3 7 Dynamite Company Museum The museum depicts the history of AECI (African Explosives and Chemical Industries), said to be the largest producer of blasting explosives in the world. It is housed in one of the original staff cottages built in 1895 on the Modderfontein Estate.

C3 8 Germiston Mainly an industrial town and railway junction, site of the largest gold refinery in the world.

B1 9 Hartbeespoort Dam The dam is a popular venue for water sports. There is also a cableway, aquarium, zoo, snake park and tea garden. Hot air balloon flights are available; transport is provided from Johannesburg.

C2 10 Jan Smuts House The modest galvanised iron and wood house of former South African prime minister and statesman, Field Marshal J C Smuts, still contains the original furnishings. There is a tea garden on site.

B3 11 Johannesburg Botanical Gardens Over 12,000 roses, herbs and exotic trees grow in these beautiful gardens.

B2 12 Kleinjukskei Motor Museum The museum comprises the largest private collection of vintage and model cars and motorcycles in the country.

C2 13 Kyalami Grand Prix Circuit Venue for the South African Grand Prix and other motor and motorcycle races.

B2 14 Lanseria Airport The annual air show in October offers aerobatics and a variety of old, new and restored aircraft.

C2 15 Lippizaners On Sundays a team of white stallions performs in the style of the famous Spanish Riding School in Vienna.

D1 16 Loopspruit Wine Cellars Although far removed from the traditional wine producing areas, a vineyard 35 km north of Bronkhorstspruit produces red and white wines. Visits are by appointment only.

A2 17 Magaliesburg Visit this small country town by steam train from Johannesburg or Pretoria.

D4 18 Marievale Bird Sanctuary On the migrant trail from north to south, the park boasts over 280 species and has three hides.

B3 19 Melrose Bird Sanctuary Extensive reed beds attract a variety of birds which can be viewed from a hide.

B3 20 Melville Koppies The small reserve of indigenous flora was the site of a Stone Age African village and iron-smelting works. It is open from September to April when guided tours are offered.

B2 21 Mzumba Dance Display Enjoy ethnic dances to the sound of African drums; South African barbecues are held at a nearby hotel.

B3 22 National Exhibition Centre The annual Rand Show held here at Easter draws great crowds.

B2 23 Organic Village Market Cottage industry products, handcrafts, jewellery and organically grown vegetables can be purchased here.

D1 24 Pioneer Open-air Museum The restored farm consisting of an original Voortrekker cottage and a reconstructed farmyard, complete with animals and farming implements, takes one back a century in time.

D1 25 Pretoria National Botanical Garden Some 77 ha of indigenous plants grouped according to climatic region of origin, provide a peaceful retreat.

D1 26 Sammy Marks Museum This beautifully restored Victorian mansion dates from 1885. Built for Marks, entrepreneur and personal friend of Paul Kruger, the house contains much of the original furniture. There is a tea garden on the premises.

C1 27 South African Air Force Museum If planes are your interest, the history of South African aviation depicted here will appeal to you.

C2 28 Transvaal Snake Park Home to a variety of African snakes.

B3 29 Wanderers Cricket Stadium Popular venue for national and international cricket matches.

D1 30 Willem Prinsloo Agricultural Museum The museum, some 39 km from Pretoria, centres around a farmstead dating from 1880, a blacksmith's shop, dairy, working water mill and a peach brandy still.

C1 31 Wonderboom Airport

C1 32 Wonderboom Nature Reserve The reserve is dominated by a 1,000 year old fig tree, 23 m high and 50 m in diameter. Small mammals and a prolific bird life occur here.

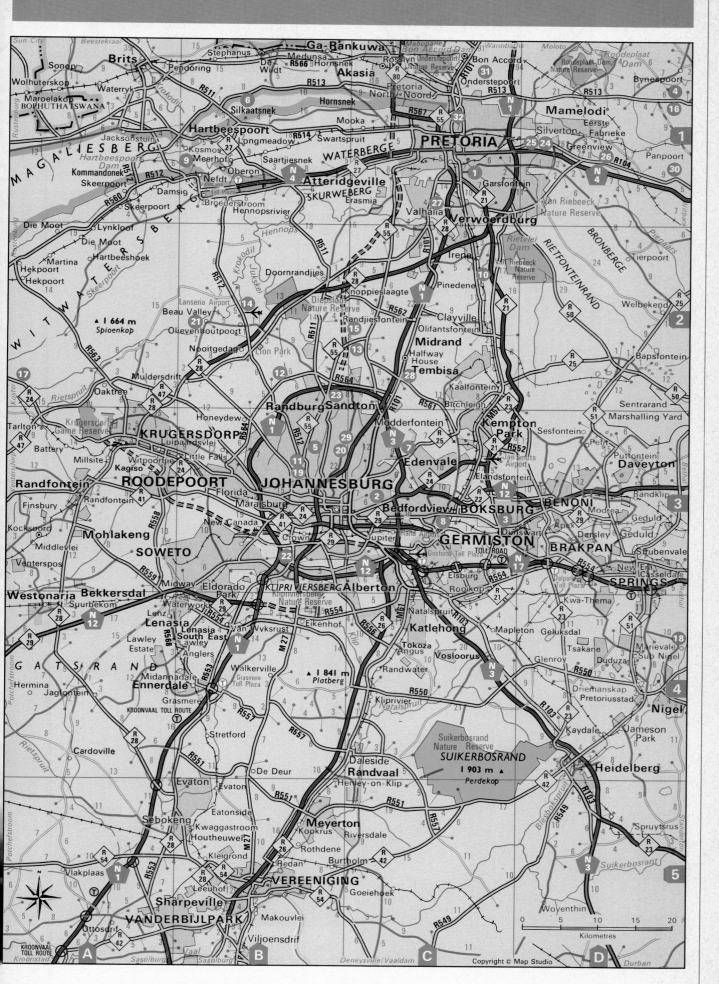

Above: *The modern, cosmopolitan metropolis of Johannesburg offers superb hotels, five-star restaurants and excellent shopping centres.*

Johannesburg

Gold was the catalyst which brought Johannesburg into being and the city's identity will always be closely linked with gold.

The chance of making big money has attracted people to the City of Gold since the early shanty town days. Many of those with initiative and drive have succeeded. Baronial mansions in the 'mink and manure belt', their grounds lined with tennis courts and fleets of Ferraris testify to the fact that Johannesburg, at the top of the supertax bracket, is a very affluent society.

This is high voltage 'nouveau riche' territory - fast paced, fun - a modern, cosmopolitan metropolis packed with vitality and verve. Superb hotels, restaurants and shopping centres pander to those with five-star tastes.

Golf courses, botanic gardens and parks are dotted about among the high-rise buildings, and the immaculately manicured gardens of the northern suburbs are worth a leisurely drive.

The city offers an exciting pleasure repertoire. Just a few of your options? Start with the sensational views from the top of the Carlton, soar to the heights in a hot air balloon, go stargazing at the Planetarium, row a boat on Zoo Lake. Tap your toes to the rhythm of township jazz, thrill to the beat of tribal drums, watch the Lippizaner stallions demonstrate their intricate routines . . .

Johannesburg has the added advantage of being within easy driving/flying distance of untamed Africa and some of the country's finest game reserves - perfect for unwinding after the pressures of nine-to-five.

Right: *The Witwatersrand has many first class golf courses within easy reach of Johannesburg and Pretoria.*

Below: *Johannesburg's glass and concrete skyline symbolises the country's escalating industrial and urban thrust.*

Left: *Gold Reef City - a replica of pioneer Johannesburg.*

Above: *Talented musicians notch up scores of accolades.*

studios in the Broederstroom area. (First weekend of the month.) See and buy the work of potters, painters, weavers, jewellers and carpenters.

Brochures providing further details and maps are available from SATOUR, Johannesburg and the Johannesburg Publicity Association.

Magaliesberg/Hartbeespoort Dam (From Johannesburg, the return trip is approximately 270 km; from Pretoria, about 250 km.)

In the Magaliesberg area, visit the largest freshwater aquarium in Africa, containing most species of South African freshwater fish, as well as crocodiles, seals and penguins. The Hartbeespoort Cable Way ride to the summit of the Magaliesberg provides memorable views. Nearby, the Hartbeespoort Snake and Animal Park are worth a visit.

From the Magaliesberg, Sun City and Lost City can be reached in less than an hour.

Sun City and **Lost City** (Bophuthatswana) offer luxury hotels, casinos, entertainment facilities and championship golf courses. Both Sun City and Lost City are enhanced by magnificent gardens. The adjacent **Pilanesberg National Park** provides sanctuary for kudu, leopard, eland, giraffe, black and white rhino, hippo, elephant, buffalo and a prolific bird life. Daily tours of the park from Sun City and Lost City.

Kruger National Park and Private Game Reserves (From Johannesburg and Pretoria, the south-western boundary of the Kruger National Park is reached by car in less than four hours; from Johannesburg, 45 minutes by scheduled flights.)

From Johannesburg, take the N1; at Pretoria turn right onto the N4. Allow time for admiring scenic highlights, in particular, God's Window and Blyde River Canyon. (Some excellent country inns are situated in the area.)

The Kruger National Park is a superlative tourist attraction, home to more species of wildlife than any other park on the continent. It supports an incomparable diversity of wild animals, birds and plants. For visitors approaching on the N4, the Malelane and Kruger gates are the most convenient. Game viewing is either by car or guided wilderness trails. West of the Kruger National Park, several privately owned reserves have been established. All of them fall within the boundaries of 'Big Five' country.

(See 'Big Game Country' page 10.)

For further information on tours and details of tour operators, restaurants, shopping centres, specialist shops and accommodation, contact your nearest SATOUR office (see back cover) or the Johannesburg Publicity Association (see page 121).

Automobile Association
Head Office:
AA House
66 De Korte Street
BRAAMFONTEIN 2001
Telephone: (011) 407 1000
AA Service: consult your telephone directory for toll free numbers throughout the country.

Below: Traditional mine dances, full of vitality and rhythm, are held at a number of venues in the city.

Suggested Tours

The following scheduled tours depart on a regular basis from Johannesburg:

Johannesburg City (including Hillbrow, Diagonal Street, Stock Exchange and African Herbalist)

Johannesburg by Night

Johannesburg Zoo by Night

The Musical Fountains of Wemmer Pan by Night

Gold Reef City

Soweto

Helicopter Tours of Johannesburg and Soweto

Premier Diamond Mine and Pretoria

De Wildt Cheetah Farm and Pretoria

Sun City/Lost City

Pilanesberg Game Reserve

Steam Train Trips to the Magaliesberg

Hot Air Balloon Flights to the Magaliesberg

Steam Train Safaris to the Eastern Transvaal

Coach tours and Fly-in Safaris to Eastern Transvaal Game Reserves

Visitors with transport have the advantage of flexibility and a great many additional options, including the following:

Arts and Crafts Studio Routes

Johannesburg Studio Route: Some art studios in Johannesburg are open to the public on the last Sunday of each month. A rare opportunity to meet the artists and craftsmen and to buy their works. Participating studios are situated in Parkhurst, Parkview, Illovo, Elton Hill and Abbotsford.

The Crocodile River Ramble encompasses 21 galleries and

Places of Interest

B3 1 Adler Museum on the History of Medicine Displays depict the history of medicine, dentistry and pharmacy in South Africa. An authentic African herbarium and witch-doctor's premises are also exhibited.

B3 2 Air Terminal A bus service operates to and from Jan Smuts Airport every half hour: 05:00-22:00.

D3 3 Alhambra Theatre This beautiful historic building in Doornfontein is a popular venue for stage productions.

A3 4 Bensusan Museum of Photography Early equipment and photographs portray the history of photography in South Africa.

A1 5 Bernberg Museum of Costume A collection of period costumes from the 18th to early 20th centuries is on display.

A2 6 Braamfontein Spruit Trail One of various urban trails incorporating places of historical, archaeological and ecological interest. The trails lead through gracious old suburbs with elegant buildings.

C4 7 Carlton Panorama The observation deck on the 50th floor of the Carlton Centre provides breathtaking views. The centre, comprising some 200 shops, and the adjacent Smal Street Pedestrian Mall form an important shopping area in the CBD. There is an ice skating rink in the centre.

B4 8 Chamber of Mines Arrangements for visits to working gold mines are made here. Booking is essential.

B3 9 Civic Theatre Watch the press for details of productions.

C3 10 Diamond Cutting Works The history of diamond recovery is depicted and demonstrations of cutting and polishing are held here.

D3 11 Ellis Park Rugby matches and tennis tournaments regularly draw thousands of spectators - 80,000 in all when filled to capacity.

A5 12 Gold Reef City This reconstruction of pioneer Johannesburg during the gold rush era, was built around a famous gold mine. Features include a Victorian funfair, brewery, pubs, hotel, restaurants, old-fashioned apothecary, Chinese laundry, tailor, newspaper office and an early stock exchange. Also see a gold pour, tribal dancing and descend an old mine shaft. Helicopter flips are available.

C4 13 Harry and Friedel Abt Jewish Museum The museum exhibits examples of Jewish ceremonial art and depicts the history of South African Judaism from the 1920s to the present.

A1 14 Hermann Eckstein Park A complex encompassing museums of military history and rock art, the zoo and **Zoo Lake** where artists exhibit on the first weekend of every month.

C2 15 Hillbrow This cosmopolitan, bustling and densely populated area is noted for its many apartment blocks, restaurants and lively nightlife. For their own safety, visitors are advised to explore in groups at night.

C3 16 Johannesburg Art Gallery Housed in an interesting building combining old and modern architecture, the museum contains a valuable collection of international and South African art. Guided tours are available. A shop and restaurant are on the premises.

B4 17 Johannesburg Stock Exchange Whether you're into stocks and shares or not, the conducted tours and audiovisual programmes are fascinating.

A4 18 Market Theatre Complex Four theatres, a bookshop, two galleries, a restaurant, bar and shopping mall make for an interesting visit. A flea market is held on Saturdays.

B4 19 Newspaper Tour View the production line of one of Johannesburg's oldest daily papers, The Star. Tours arranged on request.

A4 20 Oriental Plaza A conglomeration of Eastern traders in a bazaar-like atmosphere is encountered here. Haggling for bargains is part of the fun.

C5 21 Pioneer Park A large park which incorporates **Wemmer Pan,** popular among canoeists. It also comprises a restaurant, illuminated musical fountain, the **James Hall Museum of Transport** and **Santarama Miniland** which depicts miniature scale models of many South African features.

A2 22 Planetarium Fascinating programmes are regularly presented.

B4 23 Public Library The building comprises the main library, **Geological Museum** and **Africana Museum** which provides insight into many aspects of the history of Johannesburg.

B3 24 Railway Station Departure point for the luxury **Blue Train** to Cape Town. Make reservations at the Blue Train reservation office on the main concourse or at any travel agency country-wide.

B3 25 SA Railway Museum Old locomotives and an exhibition of model trains are on display.

C1 26 The Wilds A beautiful reserve for indigenous flora. Visitors are advised to visit the park in groups.

A2 27 University of the Witwatersrand Of interest on the campus is the statesman Jan Smuts' study which was transferred from his Doornkloof home and a collection of African tribal art in the **Gertrude Possel Gallery.**

C3 28 Windybrow Theatre This magnificent mansion built in 1896 in a pseudo-Tudor style has been declared a national monument and converted into a theatre complex. It is the Johannesburg headquarters of the drama section of the Performing Arts Council of the Transvaal.

Pretoria

Situated some 50 km north of Johannesburg, Pretoria's ambience is more sedate than that of her next door neighbour. Quieter. More appropriate to the civil servants and diplomats who live and work in the shadow of the Union Buildings. Another striking architectural landmark, the Voortrekker Monument dominates the southern skyline, symbolising the courage and endurance of the early trekkers.

Surrounded by hilly country, Pretoria is renowned for its colourful gardens, shrubs and trees - particularly beautiful in spring when jacarandas envelop the avenues in mauve.

An air of history pervades much of central Pretoria - in particular, Church Square, around which it developed. In the early days, church services were held there and it was the venue for trade and recreation. Some buildings of great historic and architectural value have been retained in the square, surveyed by a statue of President Paul Kruger.

Progress has brought in its wake high tech shopping centres, art galleries and multi-culinary restaurants. The modern State Theatre complex caters mainly for classical cultural interests: symphony and choral concerts, theatre, opera and ballet.

Within easy reach of the city centre, day walks provide a relaxing introduction to the region's natural habitats, many inhabited by indigenous animals and birds.

But if it's the slot machines you crave, the spin of the wheel and the chance of hitting the jackpot, various casinos are less than two hours' drive away.

Top: *The Voortrekker Monument commemorates the courage of the country's pioneers.*

Above: *Pretoria's up-market shopping centres offer a wide range of high quality merchandise.*

Above: *Also known as the 'Garden City', Pretoria is particularly beautiful in spring when thousands of jacaranda trees burst into bloom.*

Below: *At Verwoerdburgstad, an illuminated multicoloured musical fountain attracts visitors every evening.*

Below: *The city of Pretoria developed around Church Square, where many historical buildings have been retained.*

Suggested Tours

The following scheduled tours depart on a regular basis from Pretoria:

Pretoria City

Gold Reef City

Soweto

Cullinan Diamond Mine

Sun City/Lost City

Mabula Game Lodge

Heia Safari Ranch and Lion Park

Ultimate African One-Day Safaris

Hot Air Balloon Safaris

Visitors with transport have the advantage of flexibility and a great many additional options, including the following:

Art and Culture Routes

Wag- 'n-Bietjie Arts and Crafts Route

On the first weekend of the month, members of the public are invited to visit craftsmen and artists in several studios east of Pretoria, and to view and buy their works. Participating studios are situated in the vicinity of

Roodeplaat Dam, Cullinan, Rayton and Donkerhoek.

Pretoria Art Route

This route offers the chance of visiting a number of studios and selected galleries in Pretoria. Art works may be viewed and purchased. The route is open to the public on the last weekend of the month.

Pretoria Culture Route

The Culture Route through central Pretoria enables one to explore the city's wealth of cultural historical attractions. It includes some 48 places of interest, all within walking distance of each other.

Brochures providing maps and further details on the above routes are available from SATOUR, Pretoria and the Pretoria Information Bureau.

Pioneer Museum/Sammy Marks Museum (Zwartkoppies Hall) (Return trip is approximately 46 km from centre of Pretoria.)

Drive east along Church Street until you reach Silverton. The Pioneer Museum in Pretoria Street comprises a restored Voortrekker cottage dating back to the time when the first Voortrekkers settled on the highveld. The farmyard has farm animals and implements.

The Sammy Marks Museum is some eight kilometres beyond Silverton on the left hand side. Built in 1885, Zwartkoppies Hall was the home of Rand magnate, Sammy Marks. This grand Victorian mansion is elegantly furnished and contains one of the most valuable silverware collections in South Africa. Guided tours are available.

Willem Prinsloo Agricultural Museum/Botshabelo Open-air Museum (From Pretoria, the return distance is approximately 300 km; from Johannesburg, about 250 km.)

The Willem Prinsloo Agricultural Museum, near Valtaki, is a living exhibition of farm life in the Transvaal during the last century. At weekends, visitors can see the smithy and leatherworks in action, watch sheep being dipped and bread being baked. Demonstrations: Saturdays between 11:00 and 14:00.

Botshabelo Open-air Museum

is situated in a nature reserve about 13 km beyond Middelburg on the road to Groblersdal. It incorporates an enchanting South-Ndebele village notable for houses decorated with bold, geometric designs. You'll meet friendly Ndebele people dressed in traditional costumes of brightly coloured blankets, beads, bracelets and anklets.

Morula Sun Casino Resort (Bophuthatswana, outskirts of Pretoria.)

In addition to first class accommodation and facilities, the resort offers sundowner cruises which include grills, cold snacks and a full bar service. A bird park provides sanctuary for wild fowl and riverine birds. Canoe and walking trails enable you to study the flora and fauna.

Carousel Casino Resort (Babelegi, Bophuthatswana, 55 km north of Pretoria)

Non-stop entertainment for the entire family makes this complex with its Victorian theme a popular attraction. In addition to casino facilities, there are restaurants, coffee

shops, boutiques, cinemas and extensive children's entertainment areas.

Venda Sun (Thohoyandou, Venda, off the N1 east of Louis Trichardt.)

Set in the foothills of the Soutpansberg Mountains, the luxury Venda Sun hotel has a variety of restaurants and bars, and the casino will keep you amused far into the night. From the hotel, the northern part of the Kruger National Park is close enough for day trips.

(See also page 19 for suggested tours from Johannesburg.)

For further information on tours and details of tour operators, restaurants, shopping centres, specialist shops and accommodation, contact your nearest SATOUR office (see back cover) or the Pretoria Information Bureau (see page 121).

National Parks Board Headquarters (reservations)
PO Box 787
PRETORIA 0001
Telephone: (012) 343 1991
Facsimile: (012) 343 0905

Above: Sir Herbert Baker was the architect responsible for the creation of the Union Buildings, considered to be his greatest achievement.

Left: Flamingoes at Pretoria's National Zoological Gardens - one of the ten best zoos in the world.

Places of Interest

B3 1 A B Eksteen Transport Museum Interesting exhibits on the history of transport are displayed.

B3 2 Air Terminal and Information Centre A bus service operates between the terminal and Jan Smuts Airport.

D4 3 Anton van Wouw House 299 Clark Street, Brooklyn. The former home of the renowned South African sculptor; now a museum.

B3 4 Church Square The square, dominated by Anton van Wouw's statue of Paul Kruger, is surrounded by fine buildings. The Old Raadsaal (council chamber) in the south-western corner was the seat of government of the old South African Republic. The Palace of Justice on the northern side dates from 1898 and today houses the Transvaal Division of the Supreme Court. The adjacent building, designed by Sir Herbert Baker, was the former headquarters of the South African Reserve Bank.

B4 5 City Hall A feature of the building is the huge clock tower with a carillon of 32 bells and an organ with 6,800 pipes. The statues in front of the city hall are of pioneer leader Andries Pretorius and his son Marthinus Wessel Pretorius, founder of Pretoria.

C5 6 Fort Klapperkop A military museum which houses exhibits on South Africa's military history from the Second World War.

A5 7 Fort Schanskop One of four forts erected south of the city by the Boer forces during the Anglo-Boer War to protect Pretoria from the British. However, never used as such. Now a museum depicting South Africa's military history from the pioneer era to the time of the Anglo-Boer War.

B3 8 Jansen Collection of Africana Fine antiques and silver are on show at this small museum.

C5 9 Johan Rissik Drive A scenic drive with good views south of the city.

A3 10 Kruger House Museum The modest well-maintained official residence of Paul Kruger, a former president of the South African Republic, is now a museum. Personal belongings and relics of the period are displayed.

D4 11 Magnolia Dell This beautifully landscaped park in Queen Wilhelmina Avenue is noted especially for its magnolias. Open-air potpourri and art exhibitions are held on the first and last Saturdays of the month respectively.

B4 12 Melrose House A gracious Victorian house, venue for the signing of the Peace Treaty of Vereeniging which marked the end of the Anglo-Boer War in 1902. Now a museum containing lovely period furniture.

A3 13 Miriammen Temple The oldest Hindu temple in Pretoria, built in 1905 and dedicated to Miriammen, goddess of infectious diseases.

B2 14 National Cultural History and Open-air Museum The museum houses collections of rock engravings, fine silverware and ethnological displays. There is also an archaeological room complete with mummy. (Temporarily closed. Moving to new premises.)

B2 15 National Zoological Gardens One of the biggest zoos in the world with some 3,500 animal species in a park-like setting. A cable-car provides good views of many of the enclosures. The aquarium and reptile park accommodate fresh and salt-water fish, reptiles and a shell collection. Seals are fed at 11:00 and 15:00 and carnivores at 15:30.

B3 16 Pierneef Museum A large collection of works of this notable South African artist is displayed in the late 19th century house.

B3 17 Post Office Museum A replica of an old post office complete with antique equipment; displays depict the history of communication and there is a collection of some 750,000 stamps. (Temporarily closed.)

D3 18 Pretoria Art Museum Repository for a valuable collection of South African and international art. A library service, lectures, film shows and holiday programmes are also available.

B4 19 Pretoria Railway Station Another fine example of Sir Herbert Baker's architectural genius. A well-preserved steam locomotive is on display in front of the station.

B4 20 South African Museum of Science and Technology The museum houses well-displayed exhibits on science and technology.

B3 21 South African Police Museum Enjoy a tour of the world of crime and view relics and records of famous crimes.

C3 22 State Theatre The impressive arts complex consists of six auditoria for the staging of opera, ballet, drama, choral and symphony concerts. A flea market is held in front of the theatre on Saturday mornings.

B3 23 Strijdom Square The square commemorates the fifth prime minister of South Africa, J G Strijdom. The gigantic bust was sculpted by Coert Steynberg.

B4 24 Transvaal Museum of Natural History Excellent collections of mammals, reptiles, insects, amphibians, fossils and geological exhibits are found in the museum. The Austin Roberts Bird Hall contains a representative collection of South African birds. The **Museum of Geological Survey** is next door.

D2 25 Union Buildings The magnificent sandstone buildings designed by Sir Herbert Baker house the administrative seat of government and the national archives. Beautifully landscaped gardens and terraces in front of the buildings feature various memorials and statues. The indigenous bush area behind the Union Buildings, offers pleasant walks and a prolific bird life.

A5 26 Voortrekker Monument The monument dominates the Pretoria skyline and commemorates the Voortrekkers who left the eastern Cape in order to escape British rule. The Hall of Heroes depicts in frieze form historic aspects of the Great Trek (1838). The adjacent museum covers the same period.

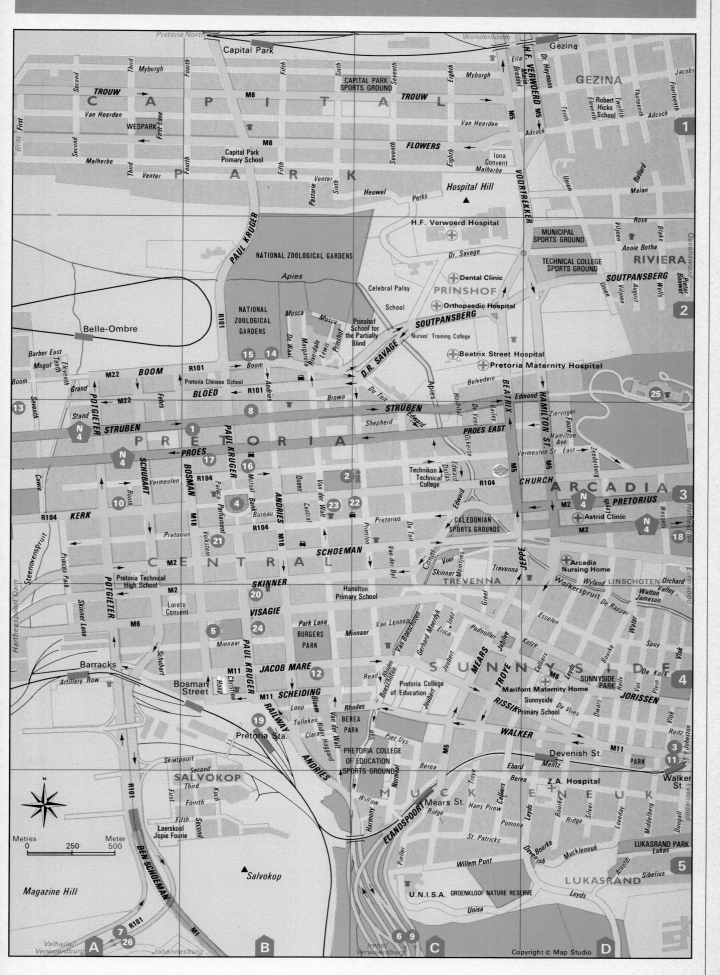

Southern and Western Transvaal

At weekends, the people of Pretoria and Johannesburg take to the road and head for their favourite getaway spots: among them, the Nyl River flood plain, the Magaliesberg and the banks of the Vaal.

In the vicinity of Naboomspruit, the sprawling flood plain of the Nyl River is a magnet for birds - and for those who enjoy identifying and admiring them. More than 400 species frequent the area, including aquatic birds attracted by the wetlands, and land birds drawn by the surrounding woodlands.

The Magaliesberg, home of colonies of Cape vultures, is another popular destination for lovers of outdoor activities such as bird watching, hang gliding, ballooning, horse riding, yachting and windsurfing. Pleasure resorts and hospitable country inns abound, and quaint craft shops invite a leisurely browse.

Westward, endless fields of maize cloak the deep and fertile plains, while small villages with peaceful homesteads enhance a pastoral landscape, once the home of Voortrekker families.

South of the industrialised Witwatersrand, the Vaal River is one of the region's most popular playgrounds. The river is always alive with bikini-clad revellers who swim, water-ski, potter around in boats or loll in the shade of sun umbrellas. Anglers notch up record catches of yellowfish, carp and barbel; holiday resorts attract an appreciative clientele, and comfortable hotels serve farm-fresh culinary fare.

For city-dwellers accustomed to tense agendas, the space and tranquillity of the region provide a welcome change.

Above: Glamorous Sun City, a jetset casino resort in Bophuthatswana.

Below: Trippers to the Hartbeespoort Dam enjoy fishing, sailing, water-skiing and hang gliding.

Above: The scenically splendid Magaliesberg attracts climbers and hikers, nature lovers, bird-watchers and horseback riders.

Below: The Vaal Dam: one of the region's most popular playgrounds.

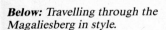

Below: Travelling through the Magaliesberg in style.

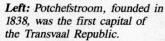

Left: Potchefstroom, founded in 1838, was the first capital of the Transvaal Republic.

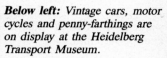

Right: Anglers notch up record catches of yellowfish, carp and barbel on the Vaal River.

Below left: Vintage cars, motor cycles and penny-farthings are on display at the Heidelberg Transport Museum.

Below right: Whiskered tern and chicks enjoying the Boksburg sunshine. These nomadic birds occur throughout the country.

Above: The hot spring at Warmbaths has been developed into a major health and holiday resort.

Left: Ndebele people are renowned for their elaborate, traditional costumes and striking mural decorations.

Places of Interest

A4 1 Barberspan The freshwater lake is the largest waterfowl sanctuary in Transvaal. Bird-watchers will delight in the more than 350 species found here.

A5 2 Bloemhof Maize centre on the banks of the Vaal River. **The Bloemhof Dam** offers good angling and other water sports. The nature reserve surrounding the dam is home to a variety of game.

C4 3 Carletonville Underground visits can be arranged to gold mines in the area. The **Abe Bailey Nature Reserve** provides a habitat for 180 bird species.

A5 4 Christiana A boom town for a while after diamonds were discovered in 1870. Relics and photographs of that era are displayed in a restaurant of a nearby mineral spa. The Vaal River offers excellent opportunities for angling and water sports.

C4 5 Heidelberg A fascinating transport museum is housed in a restored railway station dating from the old Transvaal Republic. Exhibits include vintage cars, bicycles and steam trains. A monthly steam train trip is available from Johannesburg to Heidelberg. The **Suikerbosrand Nature Reserve** in the vicinity preserves highveld plants, animals and birds although the main attraction is hiking. Day and overnight hikes are available. Booking is essential for overnight hikes.

B4 6 Klerksdorp Gold, uranium and agricultural centre. The museum houses fine cultural historical displays. The **Faan Meintjies Nature Reserve** close by is home to a variety of game.

C4 7 Krugersdorp Administrative centre of the West Rand goldfields. Of interest is the **Krugersdorp Game Reserve** and the **Preservation Centre of the Railway Society of SA** where old locomotives and rolling stock are on display. The **Sterkfontein Caves** in the district were made famous by Dr Robert Broom's discovery of the fossilised skull of a prehistoric female, popularly known as Mrs Ples. Other palaeontological finds are exhibited at the adjacent **Robert Broom Museum.**

C2 8 Lapalala Wilderness Located in the rugged Waterberg Mountains, the wilderness area provides sanctuary for a variety of plants, animals and birds. The area is the natural habitat of the rare roan antelope. Accommodation is available in chalets or camping areas. No vehicles are permitted in the area.

A4 9 Lichtenburg An attractive town in a well-watered area. Interesting exhibits on General Koos de la Rey of Anglo-Boer War fame are found in the local museum. The **Dauth-Roode** and **Centenary Dams** provide for water sports. The nature reserve on the outskirts of the town specialises in the breeding of rare and endangered animals.

A3 10 Marico District Incorporates the towns of **Zeerust, Groot Marico** and **Ottoshoop** in undulating bushveld countryside. Famous for its mampoer, a potent alcoholic brew distilled for generations from peaches, apricots and other fruit. An annual mampoer festival is held in Zeerust. The area is the setting for the tales by Herman Charles Bosman who created the literary character Oom Schalk Lourens.

D2 11 Nylstroom The town is the principal centre of the scenic Waterberg region. It is noted for its groundnut and tobacco industries, and lately for a growing grape industry which is celebrated by an annual festival each January.

D2 12 Nylsvlei Nature Reserve Located on a flood plain featuring a prolific bird life of more than 400 land and aquatic species. The reserve may only be explored on foot.

D3 13 Papatso A tribal handcraft centre comprising a replica of an Ndebele village with brightly decorated huts.

B4 14 Potchefstroom The first capital of the old Transvaal Republic, established in 1838. Many museums and old buildings depict the historic legacy of the town. **Potchefstroom Dam** offers water sports and accommodation facilities.

C4 15 Roodepoort Venue for the biennial international Roodepoort Eisteddfod. **Florida Lake** is a popular recreational area and includes the **Hamerkop Bird Sanctuary** on the western shore. A number of trails lead through the Kloofendal Nature Reserve.

B3 16 Rustenburg Centre of a farming and mining area and popular holiday destination, especially in winter. In Rustenburg Kloof there is a holiday resort with varied facilities. The **Rustenburg Nature Reserve** provides sanctuary for a variety of game and a two-day hiking trail. **Boekenhoutfontein** complex in the district features Paul Kruger's homestead and three pioneer cottages.

B3 17 Swartruggens The town serves a cattle-ranching and irrigation-farming community. The **Elandsrivier** and **Lindleyspoort Dams** are popular water sports venues.

C2 18 Thabazimbi An iron ore and platinum-mining centre in a cattle and game-ranching area. The **Ben Alberts Nature Reserve** offers game viewing and accommodation.

C4 19 Vereeniging This modern industrial town on the banks of the Vaal River is rich in coal. The **Vaal Dam** offers excellent water sports and is a popular recreation area for the Witwatersrand.

D5 20 Volksrust Historic Transvaal frontier town.

C3 21 Warmbaths Renowned for its mineral springs. The modern health complex, various resorts and game reserves attract many tourists annually.

C2 22 Waterberg Range The range stretches for 150 km through the bushveld, an area rich in indigenous trees. The southern slopes are characterised by vertical cliffs, impressive rock formations and excellent mountaineering opportunities. Cliffs known as 'Palace of the Vultures' harbour a large breeding colony of Cape vultures.

Republic of Bophuthatswana

B3 23 Pilanesberg National Park The Pilanesberg National Park, adjacent to Sun City and Lost City, offers excellent game viewing. Hunting is permitted in the safari zone of the reserve. Accommodation facilities are varied and cater for a range of tastes and budgets.

B3 24 Sun City and Lost City Two of the premier holiday resorts in Southern Africa. The upmarket complexes comprise luxury hotels, casinos, entertainment extravaganzas featuring top international stars and superb sporting facilities.

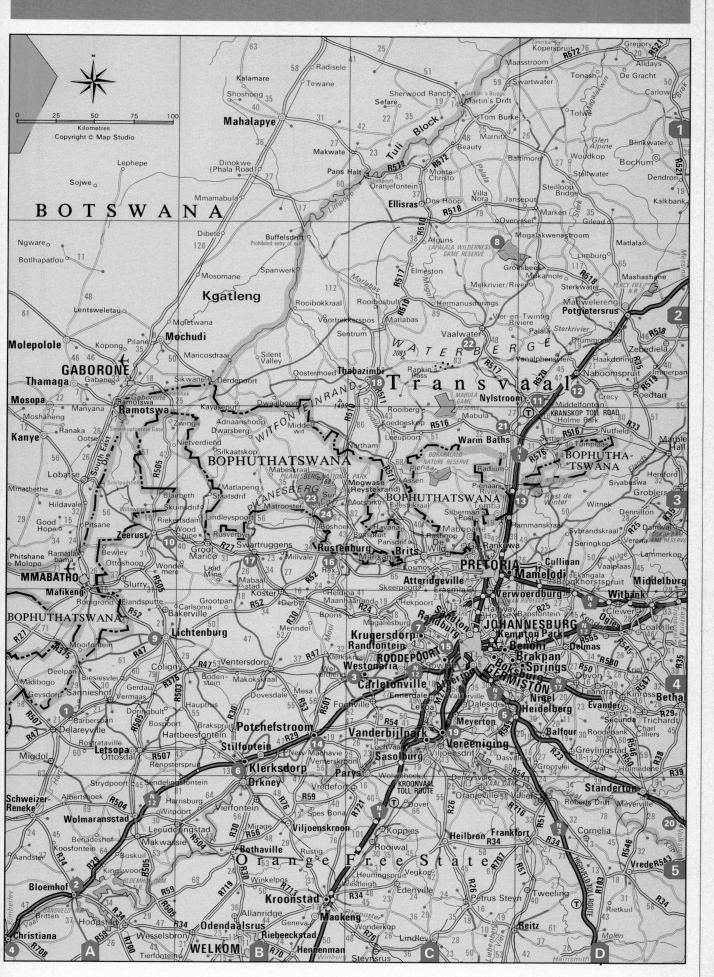

Northern Transvaal

The Great North Road from Pretoria was first carved by the creaking wheels of ox wagons. Today, when you follow the footsteps of the Voortrekkers, you'll travel on fast, safe roads, and enjoy every modern amenity as you go.

This land of legend, ruins and relics abounds in ancient forests and cycads, sparkling trout waters and cascading waterfalls. Much of the land has remained unchanged for centuries, providing sanctuary for huge numbers of game and offering unlimited opportunities for exploration and enjoyment.

Halfway between Pretoria and the Zimbabwean border, the attractive city of Pietersburg ('Capital of the North') is an ideal base from which to explore the beauty of the Magoebaskloof Pass and further afield, the thickly forested Soutpansberg Mountains, crisscrossed by delightful forest walks.

The scenic, tree-lined pass over the Magoebaskloof, between Haenertsburg and Tzaneen, winds through cool forests, fresh green tea plantations and groves of subtropical orchards.

Cradled in the southern foothills of the Soutpansberg, the picturesque town of Louis Trichardt lies in one of the loveliest regions of the country. The scenery ranks among the finest in the country and should be explored at leisure. Beyond the mountains, mopane trees and giant baobabs dominate the sweeping parklands.

While in the area, golfers should make a point of playing a round or two at Phalaborwa's Hans Merensky Golf Course, considered to be one of the finest in the country. Rumour has it that a hippo has taken up residence in one of the water hazards! Situated on the border of the Kruger National Park, the town provides an ideal base for game viewing excursions.

Above: A photographic museum is housed in this restored Dutch Reformed Church at Pietersburg.

Below: Tea pickers near Tzaneen - the centre of a fertile farming district.

Above: The scenery of the Soutpansberg region ranks among the most beautiful in the country, and should be explored at leisure.

Left: Sable antelope occur in game reserves throughout the northern and eastern Transvaal.

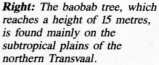

Right: The baobab tree, which reaches a height of 15 metres, is found mainly on the subtropical plains of the northern Transvaal.

Above: *Some of South Africa's finest country inns are situated in the northern and eastern Transvaal.*

Below: *Pietersburg, on the Great North Road, is the largest town in the northern Transvaal.*

Above: *Visitors to a game reserve enjoying a close encounter with black rhino.*

Left: *Venda people are noted for their attractively decorated clay pots, as well as basketware, woven articles and wood carvings.*

Right: *All dressed up to go to town!*

31

Places of Interest

B4 1 Bakone Malapa Open-air Museum Conducted tours are offered at this traditional North Sotho Bakone Kraal. An information centre provides historical background.

C1 2 Baobab This undisputed monarch of African trees occurs in large numbers in the northern Transvaal.

C2 3 Ben Lavin Nature Reserve The reserve supports a variety of game and a prolific bird life. Accommodation, camping and caravan facilities are available.

B4 4 Chuniespoort This scenic pass leads through the Strydpoort Mountains. Crocodile pools are located nearby.

C3 5 Debegeni Falls The falls consist of a series of cascades tumbling 80 m into a deep pool. Swimming is permitted but visitors are warned that rocks are slippery and dangerous.

C3 6 Duiwelskloof This picturesque village lies in a heavily wooded area. There are lovely forest drives, walks and a scenic golf course in the vicinity.

C3 7 Ebenezer Dam An attractive setting among pine forests and fine opportunities for water sports draw many visitors to the dam.

B3 8 Haenertsburg A small forestry village in an area famed for its trout streams, azaleas and Cherry Blossom Festival in spring.

D3 9 Hans Merensky Nature Reserve Many game and bird species occur in the reserve. Access is only via bus tours from the adjacent mineral spa. The **Tsonga Kraal Open-air Museum** in the reserve reflects the Tsonga way of life a century ago.

C2 10 Honnet Nature Reserve A variety of game may be viewed here. The adjacent mineral spa and holiday resort has various sports facilities, mineral pools and rheumatic pools.

C4 11 Lekgalameetse Nature Reserve Known for its mountain scenery, indigenous forests, hiking trails and large butterfly population. Fully equipped self-catering log cabins are available.

B2 12 Louis Trichardt This historic town named after a Voortrekker leader, serves a thriving farming community. Hunting and photographic safaris are available on private game ranches in the area.

C3 13 Magoebaskloof Beautiful afforested mountain pass. Scenic roads branch off the main tarred road through the kloof. Good accommodation is available in the area. **Magoebaskloof Hiking Trails,** 36 km and 28 km long respectively, traverse the region.

B1 14 Mapungubwe Hill This massive solid rock, largest of the flat-topped remains of an ancient eroded plain, provided a natural stronghold for early man.

C1 15 Messina This northernmost town in the country serves an extensive game ranching area.

C3 16 Modjadji Nature Reserve Named after the enigmatic rain queen who settled in the area in the 16th century. A forest of cycads, *Encephalartos transvenosus*, also known as the Modjadji palm, constitutes the largest concentration of a single cycad species in the world.

A4 17 Naboomspruit The area is known for its numerous mineral resorts and the scenic Waterberg Range.

A4 18 Percy Fyfe Nature Reserve A sanctuary for game such as waterbuck, kudu, impala and buffalo. The rare roan and tsessebe are bred for resettlement elsewhere.

D4 19 Phalaborwa A mining centre with rich deposits of copper, phosphate and iron. The opencast copper mine has the second largest open pit in the world. A fine 18-hole golf course borders on the Kruger Park and sightings of game are common. **Masorini Open-air Museum** in the Kruger Park, 12 km from town, comprises a reconstruction of an Iron Age village.

B3 20 Pietersburg Busy commercial centre and administrative centre of the northern Transvaal. The **Municipal Game Reserve** on the outskirts of the city accommodates a variety of game. The **Bird Sanctuary** at the water purification works is worth visiting.

A4 21 Potgietersrus Mining and agricultural centre. The **Nature Reserve/Game Breeding Centre** features indigenous and exotic game from all over the world.

B2 22 Soutpansberg Hiking Trail The trail traverses 91 km of rugged afforested terrain. Forests include exotic plantations as well as indigenous tracts featuring cycads, tree ferns, yellowwood and wild fig. Bird life is prolific.

C3 23 Tea plantations The road through the lower reaches of Magoebaskloof winds through extensive plantations. Conducted tours of the factory are offered.

B3 24 Tropic of Capricorn A column marks the point where the road crosses the southernmost tropic of the sun.

C3 25 Tzaneen This colourful town is the commercial centre of the Letaba district, known for the production of fruit, vegetables, nuts and coffee. Scenic drives lead through the area. The **Fanie Botha Dam and Nature Reserve** lie north of the town.

C4 26 Wolkberg Wilderness Area The area comprises dense indigenous forests and wide open grasslands. Bird life is prolific. Exploration is permitted on foot only.

Republic of Venda

Many places of interest are closely associated with the culture of the VhaVenda and in some cases are extremely sacred. To avoid giving offense, tourists are advised to make use of tour guides and not to venture off the beaten track without permission from Venda Tourism. Places of interest that are signposted may be visited.

C2 27 Lake Fundudzi The sacred lake, home of the python, a symbol of fertility, lies at the heart of much of VhaVenda mysticism. Permission is required to visit. The lake can, however, be seen clearly from the road winding up through the surrounding hills.

C2 28 Nwanedi National Park Well stocked with game, the park also has a prolific bird life. Accommodation and a pool are available and various dams offer good angling.

C2 29 Thathe Vondo Forest A mountain world of streams, waterfalls and forests where exotic plantations grow alongside indigenous forests. The **Vondo Dam** and the **Sacred Forest**, containing a burial place of chiefs, fall within the area.

C2 30 Thohoyandou The capital of Venda. The hotel and casino attract many tourists. A small state museum and the **Ditike** craft centre are worth visiting.

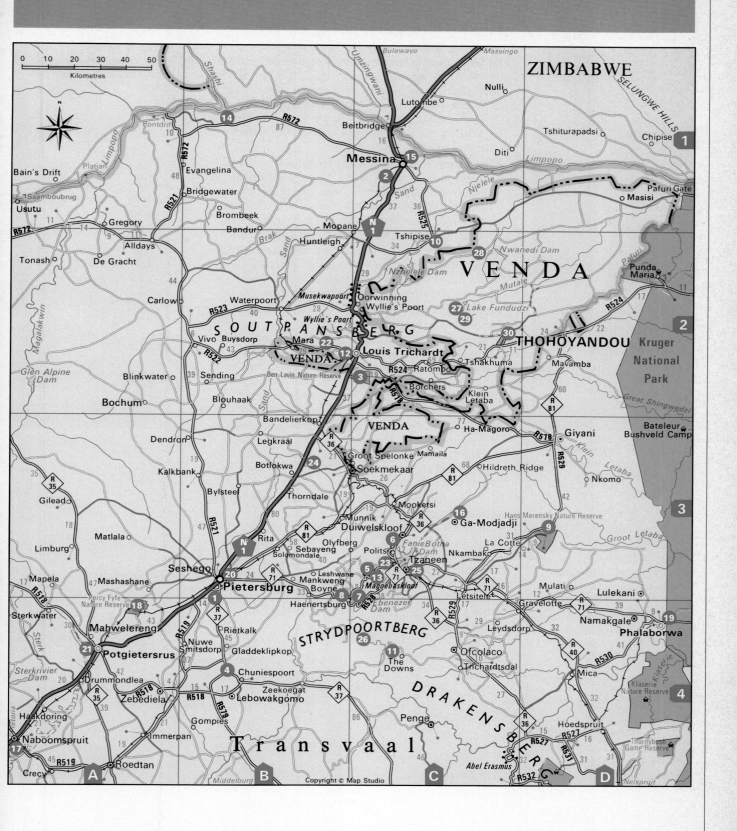

Above: *Lone Creek Waterfall plunges into a crystal-clear pool in the forest near Sabie.*

Below: *The lowveld teems with wildlife, including the 'Big Five': lion, elephant, rhino, leopard and buffalo.*

Below right: *Blydepoort Dam, set in a glorious area which offers endless opportunities for exploring and fishing.*

Eastern Transvaal

When you leave the concrete cities of the Witwatersrand behind and travel east to the brink of the highveld, the vast and airy uplands drop dramatically to rolling lowveld plains, now the site of cattle and vegetable farms, orchards, and timber, tobacco and tea plantations. At numerous roadside farm stalls, you can buy fruit and vegetables fresh from the fields.

The eastern Transvaal still has more than a hint of wildness in its glorious visual scope. Mountains, valleys, rivers, waterfalls, pockets of primal forest and a colourful profusion of flowers and birds decorate the countryside. Most of the area offers exceptional opportunities for walking, riding and fishing.

Steeped in the history of pioneers, hunters and fortune seekers, fascinating gold rush towns abound. Barberton of 'Jock of the Bushveld' fame, Pilgrim's Rest and Graskop are among the most famous.

From about 1870, the promise of gold in the region lured hardy prospectors with pack donkeys who, with courage and optimism, blazed trails over mountains and rivers, deep into the bushveld. Sir Percy FitzPatrick's international best seller: 'Jock of the Bushveld', describes his experiences when he was a transport rider plying his wagon between Barberton and Delagoa Bay (Maputo).

North-west of Graskop, God's Window provides a boundless view to eternity, stretching across miles of thickly forested mountains, the lush and fertile lowveld and the magnificent Blyde River Canyon, which ranks among the natural wonders of Africa.

The savannah lands of the lowveld teem with wildlife, offering an unparalleled experience. Track the spoor of kudu and giraffe, listen to the haunting cry of the fish eagle, roar of lion, crackle of campfire, chatter of cicada. The timeless sounds of Africa.

Right: *A greater doublecollared sunbird feasting on the nectar of a coral tree flower.*

Below: *Giraffe and zebra are perfectly at ease in each other's company.*

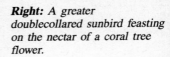

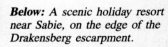

Top: *The majestic elephant is always the centre of attraction.*

Above: *Pilgrim's Rest, a living museum, is one of the major tourist attractions of the eastern Transvaal.*

Left: *Bourke's Luck Potholes, in the Blyde River - an extraordinary example of river erosion.*

Below: *A scenic holiday resort near Sabie, on the edge of the Drakensberg escarpment.*

Places of Interest

B3 1 Abel Erasmus Pass and J G Strijdom Tunnel The impressive pass connects the lowveld plains to the rugged plateau of the Transvaal Drakensberg.

B5 2 Badplaas A mineral spa offering accommodation, restaurants, shops, sports facilities and a nature reserve.

C5 3 Barberton The town developed after the discovery of gold in the area in 1884. Many reminders of these gold rush days can still be seen today.

C3 4 Berlin Falls One of various beautiful falls in the area, it plummets 80 m into a deep pool.

C3 5 Blyderivierspoort Hiking Trail The trail covers 56 km from God's Window through stunning scenery along the edge of the escarpment to the Sybrand van Niekerk Camp.

C3 6 Blyderivierspoort Nature Reserve An area of 22,000 ha incorporating the **Blyde River Canyon,** a gigantic gorge 26 km long carved out of the face of the escarpment. Accommodation is available at two public resorts within the reserve.

C3 7 Bourke's Luck Potholes This is an extraordinary example of river erosion. The deep cylindrical cavities were formed by the swirling action of flood water.

B4 8 Bridal Veil Falls The falls are reached via the scenic forest track along the south bank of the Sabie River and a ten-minute walk through dense indigenous bush.

B4 9 Dullstroom A small town in an excellent trout fishing region. A trout festival is held annually in October.

B3 10 Echo Caves Dolomite caves thought to have been inhabited during Middle and Late Stone Ages and Early Iron Age.

B4 11 Fanie Botha Hiking Trail The trail leads 80 km through beautiful scenery from God's Window to the Ceylon Forest Station west of Sabie.

A4 12 Fort Merensky and Botshabelo Mission Station The fort was built in the 19th century to protect the mission. The **Museum** and **South Ndebele Village** depict the art forms of the Ndebele people.

C3 13 God's Window A vantage point offering splendid views over the lowveld.

C3 14 Graskop A forestry village perched on a spur of the Drakensberg escarpment.

B4 15 Gustav Klingbiel Nature Reserve The reserve offers a variety of game and interesting ruins from the Late Stone Age.

C4 16 Hazyview Village served by good country hotels.

D4 17 Komatipoort The town lies at the western edge of the gorge between South Africa and Mozambique.

D1,D3 18 Kruger National Park This internationally renowned game and nature reserve, almost 2,000,000 ha in size, supports the greatest variety of wildlife species found on the African continent. Accommodation is available in 24 camps.

C3 19 Lisbon Falls The falls cascade over a sheer semicircular drop.

B4 20 Lone Creek Falls The spray over the 68-m high falls creates a rain forest effect.

B4 21 Long Tom Pass The tarred mountain pass has historic associations and offers splendid panoramic views.

A4 22 Loskop Dam Game Reserve Home to a variety of game and over 200 bird species. Accommodation at adjacent public resort.

B4 23 Lydenburg Situated in a warm pleasant valley. Well-stocked streams offer good trout fishing.

C4 24 Mac Mac Pools and Falls Crystal clear pools are suitable for swimming. The twin falls further north plunge into a densely wooded chasm.

D4 25 Malelane An agricultural area largely given to sugar cane; close to southernmost entrance to Kruger National Park.

B4 26 Montrose Falls The Crocodile River tumbles over 12-m high falls in the scenic Schoemanskloof.

B4 27 Mount Sheba Nature Reserve The Reserve embraces mountain uplands and thickly wooded ravines with rich bird life and indigenous flora.

C4 28 Nelspruit Colourful commercial core of the lowveld. The area is noted for fruit production, wayside stalls and curio shops.

B4 29 NZASM Railway Tunnel Built in 1892/3. The **Elands River Falls** and impressive **Five Arches Bridge** are close by.

B3 30 Pilgrim's Rest A living open-air museum and perfect replica of a mining town during the late 19th century gold rush. Many quaint miners' cottages and other buildings now serve as shops.

C3 31 Pinnacle Rock This massive free-standing column rises from a densely wooded gorge.

D2,D3 32 Private Game Reserves Several are situated on the western border of the Kruger National Park. All offer comfortable to luxurious accommodation and excellent game viewing.

C4 33 Sabie This charming forestry town lies in the biggest single block of man-made forest in the country.

B4 34 Sudwala Caves A series of chambers with stalactites and stalagmites. Guided tours are offered. At the adjacent **Dinosaur Park** full-scale replicas of long-extinct reptiles are displayed.

C3 35 Swadini Reptile Park Home to snakes and other reptiles.

C4 36 White River The town serves a fruit, vegetable and timber farming area.

NB Visitors to the eastern Transvaal lowveld should take anti-malaria tablets before, during and after their stay. Obtainable without prescription from local pharmacies.

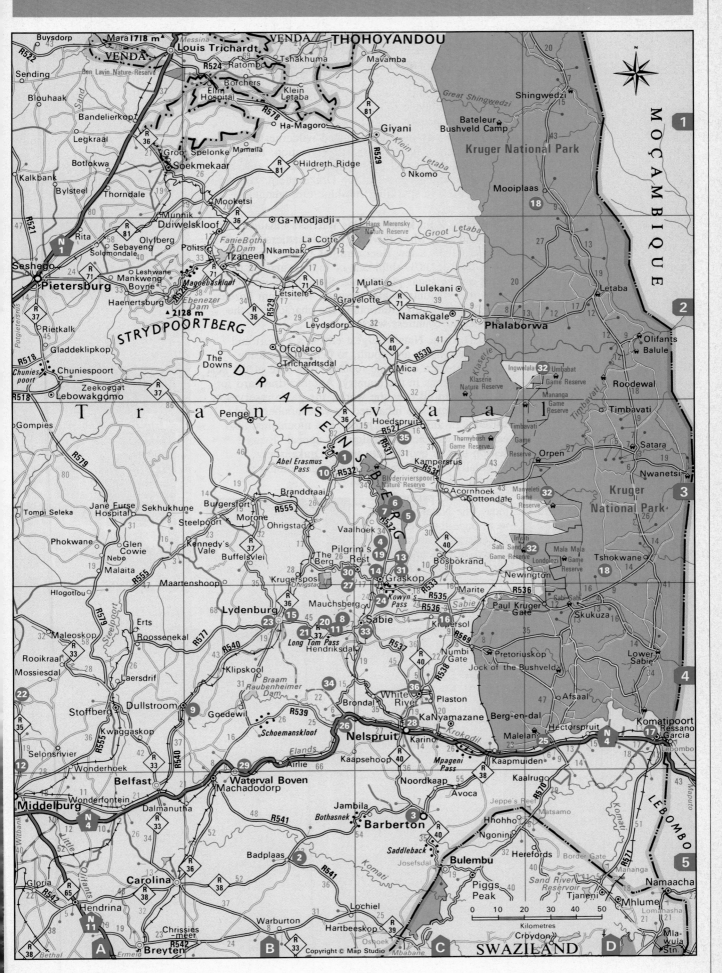

Durban

Durban offers a subtropical carnival atmosphere, endless summer, an effervescent ocean lined with golden beaches, and thousands of pleasure options.

The slogan: 'Durban - Where the Fun Never Sets' is particularly apt when applied to the Golden Mile. Sumptuous hotels command superlative views of the sea; restaurants represent every facet of the city's cosmopolitan nature; discos, night clubs and coffee bars scintillate until late. On a classical note, concert halls, theatres and art galleries pay tribute to the world's top talents - past and present.

The city is an intriguing blend of East, West and Africa. On the palm-fringed beachfront where the chic rich stroll, Zulu women sell baubles and baskets, and colourful ricksha pullers pose for photographers. Ships cruise in and out of the harbour mouth; yachts bob at anchor in the bay. And within a stone's throw of the office blocks, the theatres and shops of the business centre, you will discover a world of mosques, temples, oriental festivals and bazaars, fragrant with spice and incense. The cosmopolitan vibe is further enhanced by a constant floating tourist population.

Durban recently invested in a multi-million Rand facelift. Some roads have been converted into pedestrian shopping malls with sidewalk cafés, shrubs and palm trees; parts of the road network have been upgraded to promote an easy flow of traffic; and the main beaches have been widened and fitted with new facilities. As a result, the city's status as one of the country's top holiday playgrounds has been firmly established.

It's hard to believe that only 150 years ago, hippos wallowed among the reeds in Durban's harbour, and elephants strolled through the forests along the shore!

Top: Durban's flower market brightens up the city centre.

Above: Vasco da Gama Memorial - a familiar Esplanade landmark.

Below: The antics of dolphins enchant visitors to Seaworld.

Top: One of many attractions for children on Durban's Golden Mile.

Left: A ricksha puller, in full regalia, poses for the photographer.

Below: Vetch's Pier - a popular launching site for ski-boats.

Suggested Tours

The following scheduled tours depart on a regular basis from Durban:

City Tour

Durban by Night

Oriental Drive/Indian Market

Harbour Cruise/Sugar Terminal

Bay Cruise/Bluff Scenic Drive

Umhlanga Rocks/Japanese Gardens

KwaZulu/Umgeni Valley/Zulu Kraal

Natal Circular Drive

Natal Inland

Kranzkloof/PheZulu Tribal Village

Valley of a Thousand Hills

Umnini Craft Centre and Market at Umgababa/Crocworld

Oribi Gorge

South Coast/Wild Coast Sun and Casino

The following tours can be arranged:

North Coast/Zululand Game Reserves

Colonial Trail

Natal Battlefields

Midlands and Drakensberg Mountains

Visitors with transport have the advantage of flexibility and a great many additional options, including the following:

The Dolphin Coast (From Umdloti in the south to the Tugela River in the north.)

At a number of tranquil holiday resorts, surfing, fishing, diving, riding, hiking and golf are popular pursuits. African, Eastern and Western contrasts abound. King Shaka built his royal kraal at Dukuza (today known as Stanger). Hindu temples testify to a large Indian population. Many of the early indentured Indians settled in Verulam.

An Experience of Zulu Culture

Travel north on the N2 through sugar cane country to Eshowe. Visit Fort Nonquai (the Zululand Historical Museum) and the Vukani Missionary Handiwork Centre. Near Eshowe, three Zulu kraals (Shakaland, Kwabhekithunga and Stewart's Farm) accommodate overnight guests in authentic beehive huts, providing first hand experience of the lifestyle, rites and rituals of tribal life.

The Wilderness Experience

The return trip from Durban to the closest major game reserve (Umfolozi) is approximately 540 km. Wildlife includes white and black rhino, elephant, zebra, lion, giraffe, klipspringer, impala and kudu. Crocs occur in the rivers, and some 300 bird species have been recorded at Umfolozi. Wilderness trails lead through Shaka's old hunting grounds. A

game-viewing hide at one of the main rhino drinking pans is a major attraction. Further afield, the St Lucia, Hluhluwe, Mkuzi, Ndumu, Kosi Bay and Phinda Reserves are also well worth a visit.

(See Big Game Country: page 10)

Wild Coast Sun (Transkei: 160 km south of Durban.)

Travel south along the N2 through lush vegetation dotted with seaside resorts. Among the more popular of these are Scottburgh, Margate and Southbroom. The Vernon Crookes Nature Reserve, 15 km west of Scottburgh, and the Umtamvuna Nature Reserve, near Port Edward, provide sanctuary for a diversity of animals and birds. The Natal south coast encompasses several outstanding golf courses. All resorts have lovely beaches and first-rate swimming and fishing conditions. Transkei's Wild Coast Sun, 30 km south of Margate, on the edge of the Indian Ocean, is an up-market resort where you can swim, play tennis, golf and a number of other sports, enjoy live entertainment and try your luck in the casino.

For further information on tours and details of tour operators, restaurants, shopping centres, specialist shops and accommodation, contact your nearest SATOUR office (see back cover) or the Greater Durban Marketing Authority (see page 121).

Left: Visit the Victoria Street Market for the best selection of curry condiments in the country.

Below: The July Handicap, held at Greyville Racecourse, is one of South Africa's premier racing events.

Places of Interest

C4 1 Air Terminal Buses operate between the terminal and Louis Botha Airport on the southern outskirts of the city.

A5 2 Albert Park A trim track with jogging routes and exercise stations attracts the energetic, while the open-air chess board caters for those who channel their energy differently.

C3 3 Amphitheatre Gardens These beautifully landscaped gardens feature an open-air auditorium and sparkling fountains. A flea market is held here every Sunday. Fleamarkets are also held at Farepark in West Street (near Farewell Road) seven days a week and at the South Market Plaza at the Durban Exhibition Centre every Sunday.

D4 4 Amusement Park Dodgems and go-carts, boat rides, trips on a miniature train and aerial rides appeal especially to youngsters.

A3 5 Botanic Gardens In addition to many flowering trees, tropical plants and seasonal flowers, the gardens are well-known for the orchid house, a rare collection of cycads and the special garden for the blind with signs in braille. The tea garden is another popular feature.

C4 6 City Hall Durban's impressive city hall houses the **Public Library, Art Museum** and **Natural Science Museum.** The latter has excellent ornithological exhibits. A mummy (one of only three in southern Africa) and a life-size replica of a dinosaur, are two exhibits which never fail to impress.

C4 7 Da Gama Clock This fine example of Victorian baroque work commemorates the discovery of Natal by Vasco da Gama in 1497.

C4 8 Durban Harbour South Africa's biggest harbour has much to amuse visitors. Pleasure cruises are but one of the highlights. They depart from the Dick King Jetty. A **Maritime Museum** in a well-preserved classic steam tug next to the ferry terminal is another.

A3 9 Greyville Racecourse South Africa's most famous racecourse and the venue for one of the country's richest racing events - the Rothman's Durban July Handicap.

C1 10 Japanese Gardens Tinsley Road, Virginia. An enchanting valley of lakes, cascading waterfalls, rustic bridges and oriental lanterns.

B4 11 Jumah Mosque Reputedly the largest in the southern hemisphere and famous for its massive golden dome and turrets.

A2 12 Killie Campbell Africana Museum The original home of Dr Killie Campbell is now maintained as a museum containing three fascinating collections: the Killie Campbell Africana Library, the Mashu Ethnology Collection and the William Campbell Furniture Collection. Although visits are only by appointment, they are well worth the effort.

C3 13 Kingsmead Stadium Important sporting venue and finishing point for the Comrades Marathon every other year.

D4 14 Little Top This brightly striped landmark on South Beach stages family-type open-air entertainment each holiday season.

C4 15 Local History Museum Housed in Natal's first Supreme Court offices, this museum offers a good introduction to Durban's past and its peoples.

C3 16 Minitown The complex comprises scaled down versions of well-known Durban buildings and other features. The game park, airport and railway station are tiny masterpieces.

A1 17 Mitchell Park A shady landscaped park with children's playground, mini-zoo, numerous aviaries and a restaurant.

C4 18 Natal Playhouse Complex This ultra-modern five-venue theatre complex is the focus of performing arts in Durban. The complex has retained the façades, foyers and wood panelling of two of Durban's oldest theatres, hence the odd combination of different architectural styles.

C3 19 Old Fort and Warriors Gate Informal gardens surround the remains of a British fort that was the scene of a ten-day siege in 1842. A war museum with weaponry and memorabilia from local and foreign battles is housed in **Warrior's Gate** which is also the headquarters of the local MOTHS organisation.

B5 20 Old House Museum This historical gem depicts the lifestyle of the early colonial settlers.

A1 21 Robert Jameson Park Famous for its more than 200 rose varieties, the park is at its most beautiful in September and October.

D4 22 Sea World Aquarium and Dolphinarium Internationally acclaimed for dolphin shows in which penguins and seals feature; the fascinating variety of tropical fish, sharks, turtles and shells is also worth seeing. Shark feeding times are at 12:30 on Tuesdays, Thursdays and Sundays, so try scheduling your visits. Dolphin shows take place Mondays to Fridays 10:00-11:30; Saturdays and Sundays 10:00-11:30 and 14:00-16:15.

C3 23 Snake Park More than 60 South African species, as well as many others from overseas, are exhibited here together with reptiles such as crocodiles, iguanas and terrapins.

A5 24 Temple of Understanding Built by the Krishna Consciousness Movement, this temple off Higginson Highway in Chatsworth has been called a masterpiece of devotional architecture. The opulence of the interior must be seen to be believed. From the city the temple is reached via the Southern Freeway.

C1 25 Umgeni River Bird Park Numerous walkways and hides offer fine close-up views of brilliantly plumaged indigenous and exotic birds.

B4 26 Victoria Street Market Commonly known as the Indian Market. Experience the fun and flavour of the Orient and bargain over anything from exotic jewellery to fruit and spices.

C4 27 Whysalls Camera Museum Old and rare cameras exhibited here will fascinate photography buffs.

Copyright © Map Studio

Natal Midlands and Drakensberg

Between Natal's coastal playgrounds and the majestic Drakensberg Mountains, there is an area of gentle pastoral beauty known as the midlands. The highway meanders through rolling wooded hills and grassy plains scattered with towns, villages, hospitable country inns, and lush farmlands where plump cattle and thoroughbred horses graze.

Reserves inhabited by enormous numbers and varieties of game and birds are found throughout the midlands and the foothills of the Drakensberg. Also in the foothills, the fast-flowing rivers are especially popular among anglers who enjoy standing thigh-high in icy water, waiting for an elusive trout to catch the fly. Stop for lunch en route and you may be regaled by a tale of the giant rainbow trout that didn't get away!

The Drakensberg is the country's grandest mountain range and an ever-popular holiday destination. The slopes are alive with clear mountain streams, waterfalls, wild flowers, ferns and ancient yellowwood trees. In winter, the summits are capped with snow. Nestling in the valleys, fine hotels and leisure resorts offer comfortable (sometimes luxurious) accommodation and a broad spectrum of recreational options.

Climbers scale the jagged peaks where eagles and bearded vultures fly; hikers and horseback riders follow nature trails. If sport and holidays are synonymous in your vocabulary, you can try your hand at bowls, badminton, squash, tennis, golf, swimming and, of course, fishing. The less energetic idle away the days and admire the views from a comfortable vantage point.

Bushmen, who inhabited the caves of the area until about 100 years ago, left behind priceless records of their experiences in one of the most valuable legacies of rock art in the world.

Above: *Glorious mountain scenery, Navarone Dam, southern Drakensberg.*

Right: *One of the Drakensberg's most luxurious hotels.*

Below: *The splendid panoramas of the Drakensberg attract visitors throughout the year.*

Top: *A great way to explore the Drakensberg.*

Above: *The mountains are renowned for their beautiful indigenous flowers.*

Below: *Bushmen left a legacy of rock art in the Drakensberg.*

Left: *Al fresco art exhibition in the charming midlands village of Howick.*

Below: *Gentle, pastoral Balgowan, in the midlands.*

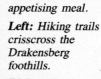

Above: *Serval in search of an appetising meal.*

Left: *Hiking trails crisscross the Drakensberg foothills.*

Right: *The elegant crowned crane.*

Places of Interest

B2 1 Bergville This village, 1,139 m above sea level, is the gateway to a number of Drakensberg resorts. A blockhouse built by British troops during the Anglo-Boer War is now a museum.

A2 2 Cathedral Peak Located at the eastern end of a spur of mountains branching off the main range, the peak (3,004 m) is thought to be the easiest of all Drakensberg summits to climb. Other peaks in the vicinity include **The Bell** (2,930 m), **Outer Horn** (3,006 m) and **Inner Horn** (3,005 m). A fascinating gallery of Bushman art can be seen in **Sebayeni Cave.**

B3 3 Cathkin Peak This prominent peak (3,181 m) is detached from the main range. The jagged pinnacle between Cathkin and the main wall is appropriately named **Monk's Cowl.**

B3 4 Champagne Castle At 3,377 m this is one of the highest peaks in the Drakensberg. Not surprising, the area offers good climbing.

C2 5 Colenso Situated on the upper reaches of the Tugela River and site of a large power station. Several major battles were fought in the area during the Anglo-Boer War. Relics can be seen in the **Robert E Stevenson Museum** next to the police station. Between Chieveley and Frere at the old Winterton turn-off is a wayside plaque commemorating Winston Churchill's role in the armoured train incident (1899) when he was taken prisoner by the Boers. A little further along the road, a turn-off leads to the **Blaauwkrantz Monument** commemorating the massacre of a party of Voortrekkers by Zulus in 1838.

B3 6 Drakensberg Boys' Choir School This world-famous choir school is situated on the farm Dragon Peaks. Visitors are welcome at scheduled performances.

C3 7 Estcourt An industrial centre in the heart of a rich stock-breeding and agricultural district. **Wagendrift Dam** is a good venue for water sports. **Moor Park Nature Reserve** at the head of the dam provides sanctuary for several species of antelope. One of many historical attractions in the area, **Fort Dunford** is now a museum.

B4 8 Giant's Castle Game Reserve One of the major reserves in the Natal Drakensberg Park dominated by a 3,000-m wall of basalt incorporating the peaks **Giant's Castle** (3,314 m) and **Injasuti** (3,459 m). The reserve serves as a sanctuary for the eland, other antelope and a variety of birds, including lammergeyer, Cape vulture, jackal buzzard, black eagle and lanner falcon. A bird-hide facilitates the viewing of cliff-dwelling species. Giant's Castle has one of southern Africa's richest stores of Bushman rock art and **Main Caves** boasts more than 500 paintings in a single, large shelter. A second shelter has life-size models of Bushmen. Accommodation is available in three hutted camps.

B5 9 Himeville Village in an area renowned for its trout fishing. A small museum and the **Himeville Nature Reserve** can be visited. An area of wetland at **The Swamp Nature Reserve** close by attracts a variety of waterfowl, including the rare wattled crane.

B4 10 Kamberg Nature Reserve (Natal Drakensberg Park) Situated in the heart of excellent trout fishing country. The Natal Parks Board's trout hatcheries are located here. A hutted camp provides accommodation.

C2 11 Ladysmith A major centre in the Natal midlands. The town was besieged by Boers for 115 days during the Anglo-Boer War and several of the most celebrated battles were fought in the vicinity. Relics of the period are displayed in the **Siege Museum** next to the old Town Hall. Water sports enthusiasts should head for **Windsor Dam** in the district.

B4 12 Loteni Nature Reserve (Natal Drakensberg Park) In addition to trout fishing, a settler museum is of interest. There is also a hutted camp.

C4 13 Mooi River An agricultural centre in an area known for its stock-breeding. **The Craigie Burn Nature Reserve** is a popular recreational area.

B3 14 Ndedema Gorge Located in the 29,000-ha **Mdedelelo Wilderness Area,** the gorge contains a fine selection of Bushman rock art.

C4 15 Nottingham Road A small town serving the surrounding stock-breeding, dairy-farming and trout fishing area. The remains of **Fort Nottingham,** built in 1856 to protect the Boers and British against plundering Bushmen, can be seen. Arts and crafts can be viewed and bought on the Midlands Meander which leads through the district (see page 48).

A1 16 Oliviershoek Pass Scenic pass with splendid views between Bergville and Harrismith.

A2 17 Royal Natal National Park Regarded by many as one of the most stunning reserves in Natal. Magnificent scenery includes the **Amphitheatre** - an eight-kilometre long half-moon shaped curve in the main basalt wall - flanked by two impressive peaks, the **Sentinel** (3,165 m) and the **Eastern Buttress** (3,047 m). The 3,282-m high **Mont-aux-Sources** lies within the park. It is the source of the Tugela River which plummets 2,000 m over the edge of the plateau. The six-hour hike up the **Tugela Gorge** is exciting. Accommodation is in a hutted camp.

A4 18 Sani Pass A spectacular winding pass up the escarpment to Lesotho on which trains of pack mules and donkeys are regularly encountered. Four-wheel drive vehicles are recommended to negotiate the pass. The five-day **Giant's Cup Hiking Trail** over 63 km starts at the foot of the pass and finishes at Bushman's Nek close to the Lesotho border.

C2 19 Spioenkop Public Resort Nature Reserve Walks with an experienced guide are offered in the game park. Boating and water sports may be enjoyed at the adjacent dam and tennis at the resort where accommodation is available. Tours of the nearby battlefields are arranged by the resident historian.

B1 20 Van Reenen's Pass The road along this sweeping pass over the Drakensberg Range drops 680 m over a distance of 15 km. The **Llandaff Oratory** in the nearby village of Van Reenen is believed to be the smallest Roman Catholic church in the world.

B4 21 Vergelegen Nature Reserve (Natal Drakensberg Park) Good trout fishing and hutted accommodation are available here.

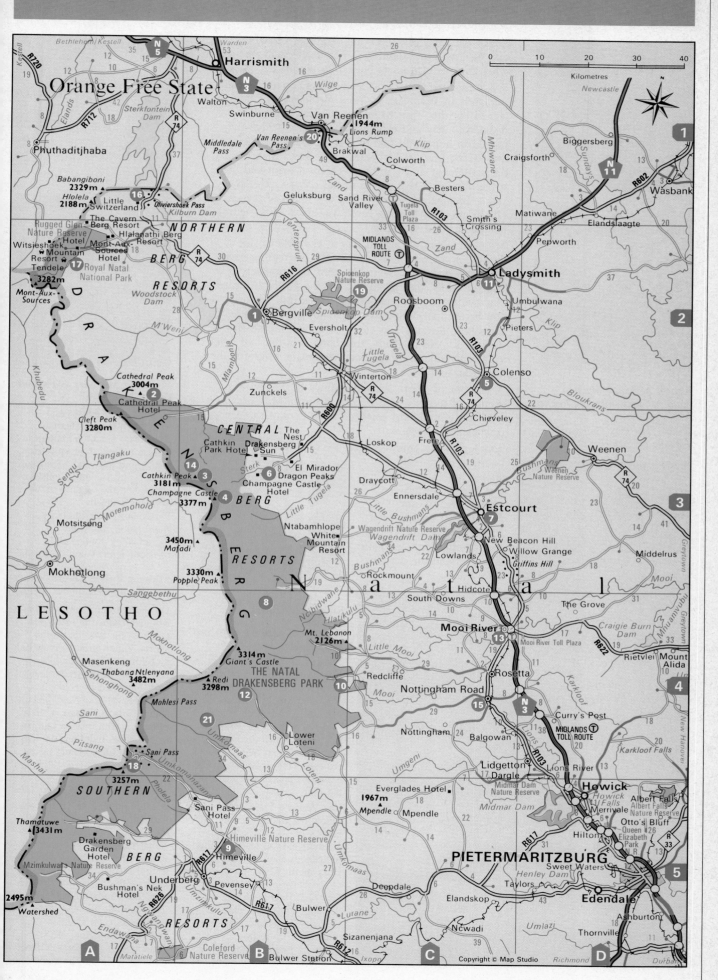

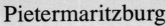

Pietermaritzburg

Set in the heart of Zulu country, Pietermaritzburg is a city of charm and dignity, at her loveliest in spring when masses of azaleas burst into bloom.

When the first party of Voortrekkers arrived in the midlands in 1837, they found a fertile tract of land ringed by hills, next to the Umsindusi River. They decided to stay and established a village which they named in honour of two of their leaders, Piet Retief and Gerrit Maritz. Six years later, the British turned the settlement into a military garrison town and made it the administrative centre of the colony. Over the years, Indians arrived and added a touch of the east: Hindu temples, Muslim mosques, spice shops, curry restaurants and silk saris.

Much of the city's appeal lies in an 'olde worlde' dignity. Numerous relics of the British regime have survived, and 'Maritzburg is often affectionately referred to as 'the last outpost of the British Empire'. Narrow, brick-paved pedestrian lanes link Victorian and Edwardian buildings. Upper crust boarding schools in the city and environs maintain elite British traditions. And in shady, tree-lined suburbs, red brick villas surrounded by spacious verandahs reinforce the Victorian ambience.

A number of Voortrekker dwellings in the older section of the city, and the Voortrekker Museum (originally a church) serve as reminders of the early trekker settlement.

Today, the city enjoys a 20th-century lifestyle, boasting top quality shops, hotels and restaurants. In the vicinity, nature and recreational resorts cater for those who appreciate the famous South African sunshine and the outdoor lifestyle.

Above: African crafts and curios: Pietermaritzburg market.

Below: The City Hall - a fine example of Victorian architecture.

Suggested Tours

Green Belt Trails (hiking and horse riding)

The purpose of the trails is to gain an appreciation of the environment. Walk slowly, stop often and tune in to nature. The trails lead through various veld types, each of which supports its own distinctive flora and fauna. Wild flowers are especially abundant in the grassland and bloom mainly in the rainy season.

The **World's View Trails** follow the route taken by early parties of Voortrekkers. The **Ferncliffe Trail** leads through indigenous forest, while the **Dorpspruit Trail,** on the banks of the Dorpspruit, has many historical links with the development of the city. Further details and maps are obtainable from the Pietermaritzburg Publicity Association.

Midlands Meander (Arts and Crafts Route)

A few artists, potters and weavers in the Nottingham Road area welcome visitors to browse around their studios throughout the week. Some of Natal's finest country inns are situated in the vicinity. A map, available from the Pietermaritzburg Publicity Association, indicates participating studios and provides information on hotels.

Midmar Public Resort Nature Reserve and Historical Village

On the northern shore of the Midmar Dam, the resort has facilities for land and water sports. Other attractions include a children's playground, a restaurant, riding trails, and a park inhabited by rhino, antelope, zebra and wildebeest. The historical village, a 'living museum', comprises a number of old Natal buildings depicting aspects of life in Natal in the early days.

Battlefields of Northern Natal

A large number of significant battles on South African soil took place in northern Natal. Pietermaritzburg is a gateway to these battlefields which lie within a small area between Ladysmith and Newcastle and the Zulu capital of Ulundi. They include Blood River battlefield, near Dundee: trekkers and Zulus, 1838; Isandhlwana and Rorke's Drift battlefields, near Dundee:

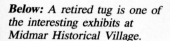

Left: Concrete office blocks rub shoulders with buildings from a bygone era.

***Right:** Pietermaritzburg's mosques indicate the presence of a large muslim community.*

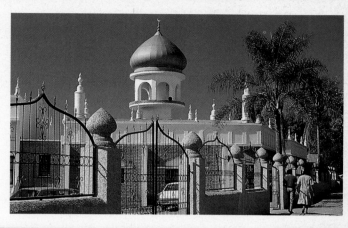

***Below:** A retired tug is one of the interesting exhibits at Midmar Historical Village.*

Anglo-Zulu War, 1879; Ulundi battlefield, KwaZulu: Anglo-Zulu War 1879. Details of the Northern Natal Battlefields Route are obtainable from the Talana Museum just outside Dundee.

The Wilderness Experience

Game Valley, a popular wildlife resort 19 km from Pietermaritzburg in the Karkloof Valley, is inhabited by a great diversity of game and bird life.

From Pietermaritzburg, Giant's Castle Game Reserve in the Drakensberg is situated some 70 km south-west of Estcourt. Wildlife includes 12 species of antelope, and the reserve is an excellent bird-watching area. Further afield, the Royal Natal National Park and Itala Nature Reserve are well worth a visit.

For further information on touring regions, restaurants, shopping centres, specialist shops and accommodation, contact your nearest SATOUR office (see back cover) or the Pietermaritzburg Publicity Association (see page 121).

Natal Parks Board Headquarters (reservations)
PO Box 662
PIETERMARITZBURG 3200
Telephone: (0331) 47 1981
Facsimile: (0331) 47 1980

***Above:** Pietermaritzburg's charm is enhanced in spring by masses of azaleas in bloom.*

***Left:** Karkloof Falls - a popular site for picnickers and sightseers.*

Places of Interest

D1 1 Albert Falls Public Resort and Nature Reserve The attractive horseshoe-shaped falls, some 18 km north of the city, are spectacular in the rainy season. A dam offers sailing, powerboating, water-skiing and fishing. Chalets and a caravan park provide accommodation.

B4 2 Alexandra Park This 65-ha landscaped park is noted for the magnificent pavilion with its intricate iron and latticework and the equally impressive bandstand. Both date from the 1890s. The park is the venue for the annual art exhibition, **Art in the Park,** in May. A flea market is held on the first Sunday of each month. The park is also the starting point of the annual **Duzi Canoe Marathon** which takes place over a distance of 138 km to the Blue Lagoon in Durban.

A4 3 Botanic Gardens Comprising two distinct sections, the gardens feature exotic and indigenous plants. A tearoom provides refreshments.

B3 4 City Hall The ornate red brick building which has aptly been called a tribute to Victorian design, features a 47-m high clock tower, a 12-bell carillon, domed rooftops, stone carvings and beautiful stained glass windows. It is reputed to be the biggest all-brick building in the southern hemisphere. Every other year, it is the starting point of the Comrades Marathon between Durban and Pietermaritzburg on May 31. In other years the marathon starts in Durban and finishes at Jan Smuts Stadium in Pietermaritzburg.

D4 5 Comrades Marathon House Museum A restored Victorian house where memorabilia of this famous marathon are displayed.

C2 6 Hindu Temple The Sri Siva Soobramonair and Mariammen Temple is the main place of worship for the city's Hindu population. On Good Friday devotees mark the end of a fast by walking barefoot across glowing coals. A fireworks festival is also held at this time.

A1 7 Howick Falls The 100-m high falls are the focus of the **Umgeni Valley Nature Reserve** which accommodates a variety of wildlife. Bird-watching is excellent and over 200 species have been recorded.

C2 8 Islamia Mosque Visitors are allowed access to the largest mosque in the city.

A4 9 Macrorie House Museum This charming house museum providing fascinating glimpses into the elegant Victorian lifestyle of the early British settlers, was the home of Bishop William Macrorie from 1869 to 1891.

B3 10 Natal Museum One of five national museums in the country; houses excellent displays, notably in the 'Hall of Natal History' which depict Pietermaritzburg as it was in the 1850s.

B3 11 Old Colonial Building The soaring columns of this fine building reflect the architecture of the late 19th century. Completed in 1899, it housed various departments of the Natal Colonial Government.

A4 12 Old Government House Built in the 1860s, the building was the home of Lieutenant-Governor Sir Benjamin Pine who later sold it to the Natal Government for use as an official residence for the colony's governors. It is now a national monument.

B3 13 Old Supreme Court A fine example of colonial architecture which formed the centre of the capital's defensive system during the Anglo-Zulu War of 1879. A major attraction today is the **Tatham Art Gallery** which houses a collection of late 19th- and early 20th-century paintings as well as exhibits of china, glassware and clocks.

C5 14 Oribi Airport An air service operates between Margate, Pietermaritzburg and Jan Smuts (Johannesburg).

B3 15 Publicity House Built in 1884 for the Borough Police, this is another of Pietermaritzburg's red-brick national monuments. It now houses the Pietermaritzburg Publicity Association.

A2 16 Queen Elizabeth Park Headquarters of the Natal Parks Board, the park (signposted) offers picnic spots and lovely walks.

A4 17 Railway Station Another fine red-brick building dating from the Victorian era, noted especially for its contrasting stone facings and the cast-iron lacework on the huge verandah.

D4 18 Scottsville Racecourse An important national horse racing venue.

A3 19 Victorian House One of several gracious Victorian houses in the city which have been declared national monuments. Because many of these buildings are either private homes or office buildings, they may only be viewed from the outside. Details on other buildings are available from the Publicity Association.

B3 20 Voortrekker House The oldest surviving double-storey Voortrekker house in the city. Restored and furnished with period furniture. The yellowwood ceilings and wood-tiled floors are fine examples of early Voortrekker craftmanship.

B3 21 Voortrekker Museum and Memorial Church The Church of the Vow was built by the Voortrekkers after their victory over the Zulus at the Battle of Blood River in 1838. It was converted into a museum in 1912 and houses a collection of Voortrekker relics, including an ox wagon and an ironwood chair said to have belonged to the Zulu king Dingaan. The restored home of the hero of the Battle of Blood River, Andries Pretorius, is next to the museum.

A2 22 World's View A 305-m high vantage point (signposted) offering spectacular views of the city and surrounding area. The old wagon road below the viewsite which was used by the early Voortrekkers after crossing the Drakensberg to reach Port Natal (later Durban), now forms part of Pietermaritzburg's system of Green Belt Trails.

A2 23 Wylie Park The park in Taunton road, off Howick Road, is one of several luxuriant public parks in the city. Although given largely to indigenous plants such as proteas and heaths, azaleas (the floral emblem of Pietermaritzburg) also grow in profusion and provide a spectacular sight in spring.

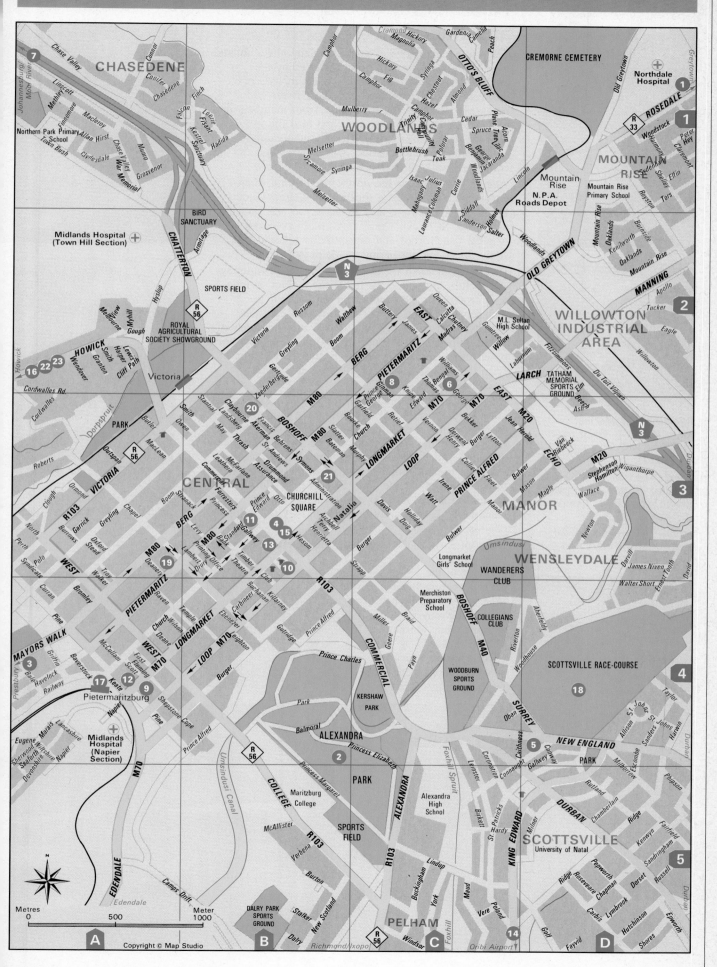

Natal North Coast and Interior

The game sanctuaries of northern Natal and Zululand were designed for nature-lovers who enjoy the untamed African wilderness. Habitats include open bushveld, coastal dune forests, lakes, rivers and mangrove swamps. Animals range from members of the 'Big Five' to the tiny suni, and bird life is prolific. Most parks offer peaceful surroundings, comfortable accommodation, game drives and conducted walking trails.

Anglers converge on the northern coastline where game fishing provides a thrilling challenge. Good fishing conditions are also found in the lake and estuary of St Lucia. Coral reefs, multi-coloured tropical fish, turtles and rays provide a fascinating study for scuba divers and snorkellers.

Richards Bay has beaches for fishing and swimming, yacht clubs and attractive resort areas. Not so long ago, crocodiles and hippos had the harbour to themselves. Today, the port is a hive of constant activity, with trains bringing coal from the Transvaal to the ships in the harbour for export. Tour operators based in the area will arrange to transport visitors from the Richards Bay Airport to major game reserves.

The coastline stretching from the Tugela Mouth to the Umhlanga River is aptly known as the Dolphin Coast. Close inshore, shoals of bottle-nosed dolphins play in the waves, providing endless entertainment with their engaging antics. Thanks to a sunny climate and mild seas, the tranquil holiday retreats in the area attract visitors throughout the year. South of Umdloti, Umhlanga Rocks has top quality hotels and restaurants, broad sandy beaches and stylish shopping centres.

Many of KwaZulu's unsung features are found in rural areas far from the glamour of the cities. Travellers on a flexible itinerary should branch off the highway to explore. Your journey will be enriched by an experience of Africa virtually unchanged since the beginning of time.

Top: Holiday chalet at Sodwana Bay - a major resort for fishing and diving enthusiasts.

Above: Many antelope species, including the distinctive nyala, inhabit Mkuzi Game Reserve.

Below: The northern coastal resorts cater for those who enjoy silence and solitude.

Above: In the rolling hills of Zululand, sangomas throw the bones . . .

Left: *Exploring Sodwana's fascinating underwater world.*

Right: *St Lucia is renowned for its prolific bird life.*

Below: *Conducted bushveld trails feature on the programme at Mkuzi Game Reserve.*

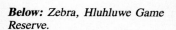

Above: *North of Durban, Umhlanga Rocks attracts holiday-makers all year round.*

Right: *What a lazy way to spend the day! Hippo, St Lucia Complex.*

Below: *Zebra, Hluhluwe Game Reserve.*

Right: *White rhino are found in many of northern Natal's game reserves.*

53

Places of Interest

C3 1 Ballito This up-market holiday resort has shark-protected beaches, a tidal pool and paved promenade.

B2 2 Blood River Monument Full-scale bronze replicas of wagons mark the site of the Battle of Blood River (16 December 1838) where the Voortrekkers with a force of 464 men defeated a Zulu impi (regiment) of 12,000.

B2 3 Dundee Capital of the northern Natal coalfields. The fascinating **Talana Museum** incorporates a Victorian farmstead, a miner's house and other interesting exhibits.

C2 4 Empangeni Commercial centre of the area and of the sugar industry. The **Enseleni Nature Reserve** offers game viewing. Four trails lead through the park.

C3 5 Eshowe A colourful town ablaze with flowering trees and shrubs surrounded by the **Dlinza Forest Nature Reserve** where small mammals and many birds occur. **Shakaland, Kwabhekithung Kraal** and **Stewart's Farm** recapture the traditional Zulu way of life and offer accommodation.

C2 6 Hluhluwe Game Reserve One of the oldest game reserves in the country, noted especially for its black and white rhino. The reserve is also inhabited by lion, elephant, buffalo, giraffe, leopard, cheetah, hippos, crocodile and various antelope species. Hutted accommodation provides overnight facilities. A restaurant is available.

B2 7 Isandhlwana A monument marks the site of the battle fought here in January 1879 between British forces and Zulu warriors. There is a small museum on site.

D1 8 Kosi Bay Nature Reserve The reserve comprises a network of lakes with mangroves, rare orchids, raffia palms and a wealth of aquatic birds. Because of the presence of hippos and crocodiles, swimming is not recommended. Accommodation is available in a camp with campsites and thatched lodges.

D1 9 Lake Sibaya Largest freshwater lake in the country and home to about 160 hippos and many Nile crocodiles. A picturesque rustic camp provides accommodation.

A1 10 Majuba Site of battle between Boer and British forces on 27 February 1881. At O'Neill's cottage close by, an agreement was signed to end hostilities.

D1 11 Mkuzi Game Reserve Enjoy good game viewing in this land of fever trees and fossil remains. A hide at Nsumu Pan provides excellent bird-watching. There are chalets and camping sites.

C3 12 Mtunzini An attractive resort in parklike surroundings. The **Umlalazi Nature Reserve** is an area of coastal dunes and swamps inhabited by numerous antelope species and many birds. Self-catering accommodation is available. The raffia palms south of the reserve have been declared a national monument.

D1 13 Ndumu Game Reserve A network of pans on a flood plain supports a fascinating variety of fish, bird and animal species. Many tropical East African birds are encountered here as the reserve is the limit of their southern range. Other attractions include hutted accommodation, game-spotting drives and walks.

A1 14 Newcastle A major centre for the production of steel and textiles. There are many battlefields in the area,

hiking trails and the **Fort Amiel Cultural and Historical Museum.**

B1 15 Paulpietersburg A centre for coal-mining and timber cultivation. The **Pongola Bush Nature Reserve** embraces a valuable area of indigenous evergreen forest. Visits must be arranged beforehand with the Officer-in-Charge in Vryheid. There are various hiking trails in the area.

C2 16 Richards Bay South Africa's largest and busiest harbour. Guided tours are available. The **Richards Bay Nature Reserve** is a popular angling venue with a prolific bird life.

B2 17 Rorke's Drift At this important Anglo-Zulu War battlefield, there is today a tribal arts and craft centre.

D2 18 St Lucia Game Reserve/Greater St Lucia Wetland Park A complex of lakes, dunes and beaches consisting of different reserves around Lake St Lucia. Bird life is prolific and there are many crocodiles and hippos. Accommodation is available in hutted camps.

C3 19 Salt Rock The rugged coastline offers good fishing.

C3 20 Shaka's Rock Resort with a secluded beach and tidal pool.

C3 21 Sheffield Beach, Blythedale Beach and Zinkwazi Mouth Small unspoilt resorts with beaches protected by shark nets.

D1 22 Sodwana Bay National Park This park is a paradise for fishermen and divers and has overnight facilities.

C3 23 Tongaat Beach Besides safe bathing, **Crocodile Creek,** where these reptiles are bred and conserved, may be visited.

C2 24 Ulundi The capital of KwaZulu. The **KwaZulu Cultural Museum** houses interesting displays relating to Zulu history, regional cultural history and archaeology.

B3 25 Umdloti At this small but popular resort, shark nets and a tidal pool make for safe bathing.

C2 26 Umfolozi Game Reserve In addition to white and black rhino, a variety of game occurs here. Wilderness trails through the reserve are in great demand. Hutted accommodation is provided.

C2 27 Umgungundhlovu Site of the royal town of the 19th century Zulu king, Dingaan. At **KwaMatiwane,** the Voortrekker leader, Piet Retief, and his men were killed on Dingaan's orders. The huts of the royal quarters have been reconstructed and may be viewed. Fascinating archaeological finds are displayed in the museum.

B3 28 Umhlanga Rocks Up-market resort with sophisticated shopping malls, a beach with sandy stretches and rocky areas, and a paved walkway along the beach. Trails meander through the dune forest of the **Umhlanga Lagoon Nature Reserve.**

B1 29 Vryheid Decisive battles were fought in the vicinity during the Anglo-Boer War. Today the town serves a coal-mining and cattle-ranching area. The museum houses interesting displays.

NB Visitors to northern Natal should take anti-malaria tablets before, during and after their stay. Obtainable without prescription from local pharmacies.

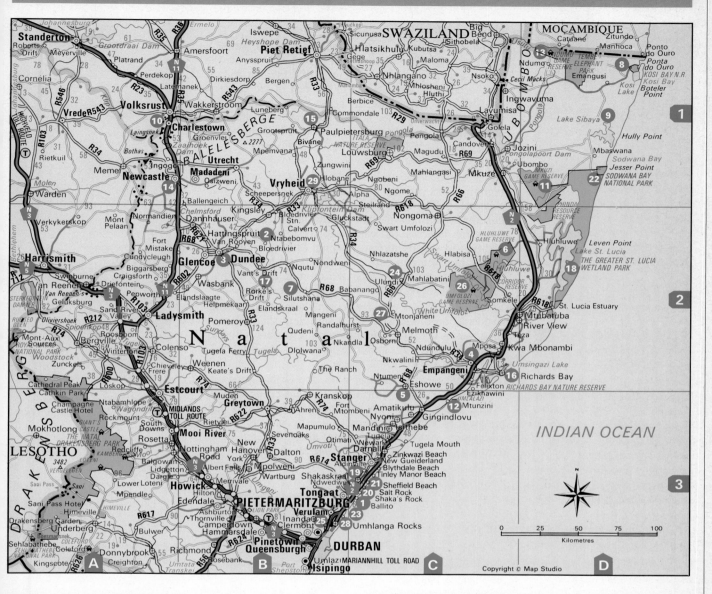

B3,D1   Private Game Reserves   Several are situated in northern Natal and the midlands. They offer comfortable accommodation and excellent game viewing.

C1   Itala Game Reserve   The reserve just north of Louwsburg is scenically beautiful and offers a variety of habitats. Game includes elephant, black and white rhino, buffalo and cheetah. Three-day wilderness trails are available from March to October. A hutted camp, bushcamps and a camping site provide accommodation.

Further information on attractions and facilities in KwaZulu is available from:
KwaZulu Bureau of Natural Resources
Private Bag X23
Ulundi
3838
Telephone: (0358) 20 2711/20 2664
Facsimile: (0358) 20 2660

Natal South Coast and Interior

Throughout the year, holiday-makers flock to their favourite south coast haunts to cultivate a tan, ride the waves, eat, drink and generally jollify. In June and July, especially, when much of the rest of the country dons its winter woollies, the south coast is definitely the place to be! Winter is also the time when huge shoals of sardines swim close to shore, bringing in their wake game fish, dolphins and thousands of hungry sea birds.

From Amanzimtoti to Port Edward, the N2 coastal highway links popular seaside resorts in rapid succession. The road snakes through subtropical bush, canefields and hills garlanded with hibiscus blooms. Sweeping beaches and calm lagoons abound, and in addition to superb surfing, fishing, boating and swimming, you can play golf, bowls and tennis, visit a croc farm and while away the evening at a cinema. Many shops open on Sundays and public holidays.

Some resorts have massive rocks where anglers stand endlessly on the lookout for a succulent shad. Some have waves that are legendary among surfers. Others appeal to those who prefer to laze away the days in peace on a sun-splashed beach.

For a change from sea and sand, the Oribi Gorge Nature Reserve is a little Eden of giant cliffs, forests, rivers, rapids and ravines. In the reserve, visitors can follow a baboon viewing trail. Nearby, at Port Shepstone, you can catch a ride on the Banana Express, Natal's last narrow gauge steam train. It twists, winds, climbs and sometimes almost doubles back on itself as it negotiates the hills and valleys of the countryside.

Just across the Transkei border, the Wild Coast Sun offers diversions of a more sophisticated kind - one armed bandits, gambling tables and live entertainment.

Above: *Oribi Gorge Nature Reserve - a scenic masterpiece.*

Top: *Boating on the lagoon is among a wide range of leisure options at Ramsgate.*

Above: *On the south coast, you can cultivate a tan, even in winter.*

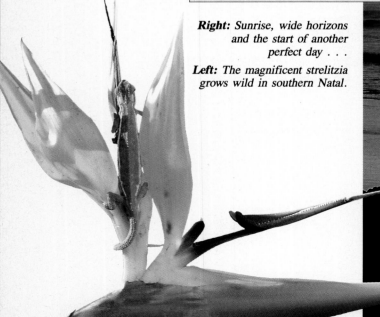

Right: *Sunrise, wide horizons and the start of another perfect day . . .*

Left: *The magnificent strelitzia grows wild in southern Natal.*

Left: *Holiday-makers flock to Margate to sunbathe, ride the waves, eat, drink and generally jollify.*

Below: *African crafts and curios are sold at Umgababa, on the south coast.*

Left: *Anglers on the lookout for a succulent shad.*

Below: *The Umtamvuna River forms the boundary between Natal and Transkei.*

Above: *An up-market resort on the lower south coast.*

Places of Interest

C3 1 Amanzimtoti Nyoni Rocks is the most popular section along this superb seven-kilometre long beach. Restaurants, a mini waterworld and a saltwater filtered pool are found there. Places of interest include the bird sanctuary and the **Ilanda Wilds Nature Reserve** which is noted for its prolific bird life.

B4 2 Bendigo The town comprises the four seaside villages of **Sunwich Port, Anerley, South Port** and **Sea Park.** Sunwich Port offers excellent bathing in the sea and good angling at Domba Bay, Anerley has a tidal pool, South Port safe bathing and Sea Park a beach which is popular mainly among anglers.

B4 3 Hibberdene A bathing beach, an amusement complex on the north bank of the lagoon and boating facilities on the Mzimayi River are some of the attractions here. At **Umzumbe** there is safe bathing and kite angling at Stiebel Rocks. The small, safe beach at **Banana Beach** is surrounded by indigenous shrubs.

B4 4 Ifafa Beach A popular angling resort at the mouth of the Ifafa River with an impressive lagoon which is ideal for water-skiing, canoeing and angling. **Mtwalume** has a bathing beach, a tidal pool and good angling opportunities along its rocky coastline.

C3 5 Kelso, Umdoni Park and Pennington Small peaceful resorts for caravanners, anglers, spear-fishermen and scuba divers.

D3 6 Kingsburgh The five seaside resorts of **Karridene, Warner Beach, Winklespruit, Illovo** and **Doonside** make up this town. All offer safe bathing and offshore shark nets and are especially noted for their wide stretches of sand and gentle lagoons.

B5 7 Margate This popular resort with its many restaurants, discos and live cabaret is particularly favoured by the young. Besides shark-protected beaches and good fishing, especially from the fishing pier south of the main beach, attractions include an amusement park, bowling alley, 18-hole golf course and skating rink. In peak season beauty competitions and variety shows are held on the beach. An air service operates between Margate and Jan Smuts Airport in Johannesburg via Pietermaritzburg.

B5 8 Marina Beach A lovely spacious beach protected by shark nets. A tidal pool and lagoon are found at this small resort which adjoins the private, very up-market resort of San Lameer.

A4 9 Oribi Gorge Nature Reserve High sandstone cliffs dominate this 24-km long gorge carved out by the Umzimkulwana River. Leopards, troops of baboons, various small antelope and a prolific bird life, including five species of kingfisher and seven species of eagle, occur here. There are several nature trails and accommodation is available in a hutted camp.

A5 10 Port Edward The most southerly coastal resort of Natal. Although small and peaceful, offering safe swimming and excellent fishing, it also attracts many visitors on account of the proximity of the Wild Coast Sun Casino. The **Umtamvuna Nature Reserve** south of the town is noted for its bird life and many rare and protected plant species.

B4 11 Port Shepstone Here, visitors enjoy good beaches, a tidal pool, an 18-hole golf course and other sports facilities. The Umzimkulu River is navigable in small craft for a distance of eight kilometres upstream.

B5 12 Ramsgate In addition to fine bathing facilities and a lagoon where boat rides are offered, the resort has restaurants, antique shops and galleries. **Ski Boat Bay** is a popular venue for the ski-boat fraternity.

B5 13 St Michael's on Sea Safe bathing, golf, bowls, and a tidal pool are available. Canoes and paddle-boats may be hired at the tearoom across the lagoon.

C3 14 Scottburgh The rugged coastline offers excellent fishing, especially off Aliwal Shoal. The main beach has shark nets and a tidal pool. A miniature railway and supertube amuse tiny tots. **Crocworld,** close by, breeds and conserves crocodiles.

B5 15 Shelly Beach Named after the many shells found here. Safe bathing and good angling may be enjoyed.

B5 16 Southbroom The coastline consists of a series of rocky bays. Two sheltered lagoons provide for boating and board-sailing, while the beach at the Mbizane Lagoon is protected by shark nets. The 18-hole golf course is popular among residents and visitors alike. The **River Bend Crocodile Farm** is close by.

A5 17 Trafalgar Marine Reserve The marine fossil beds in this reserve are the only such beds in South Africa and are of great archaeological value. The reserve stretches from the highwater mark to 500 m out to sea. Fishing is allowed but not the collecting of bait.

C3 18 Umkomaas The rocky coastline provides fine fishing but prohibits sea bathing. There is, however, a lovely tidal pool in addition to facilities for tennis, bowls and golf.

B4 19 Umtentweni The main beach, protected by shark nets, nestles between a strip of coastal forest and the sea. A tidal pool and numerous rock pools also await visitors here.

B5 20 Uvongo Just before the Ivungu River reaches the sea, it narrows into a rocky gorge before spilling 23 m down a waterfall into a lagoon, forming one of the deepest estuaries in the country. In addition to safe bathing in the sea, there is a tidal pool, children's paddling pool and boats for hire on the lagoon. Fishing opportunities are good, especially at Orange Rocks, Beacon Rocks and La Crete Point. **Manaba Beach** offers fine fishing at Shad Bay, a tidal pool and rock-enclosed private beaches.

B3 21 Vernon Crookes Nature Reserve Prolific numbers of bird species, and game such as eland, zebra, blue wildebeest and nyala make this a popular visiting place. The hutted camp makes for a comfortable stay-over.

A5 22 Voortrekkerstrand This resort incorporates **Glenmore** with its safe beach and lagoon and the tranquil resorts of **Leisure Crest** and **Leisure Bay.**

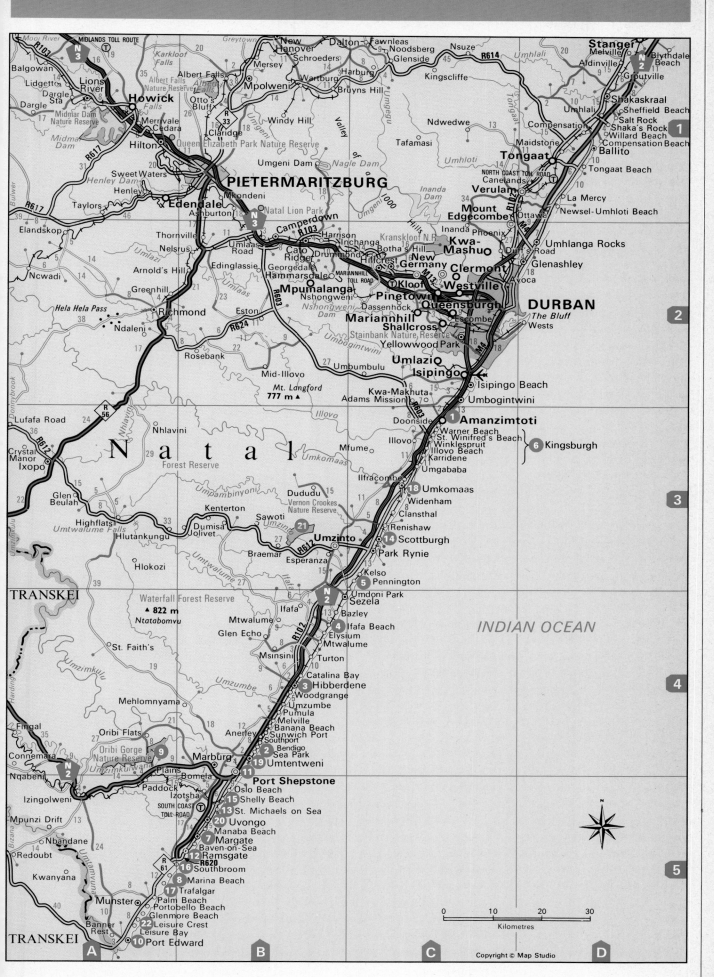

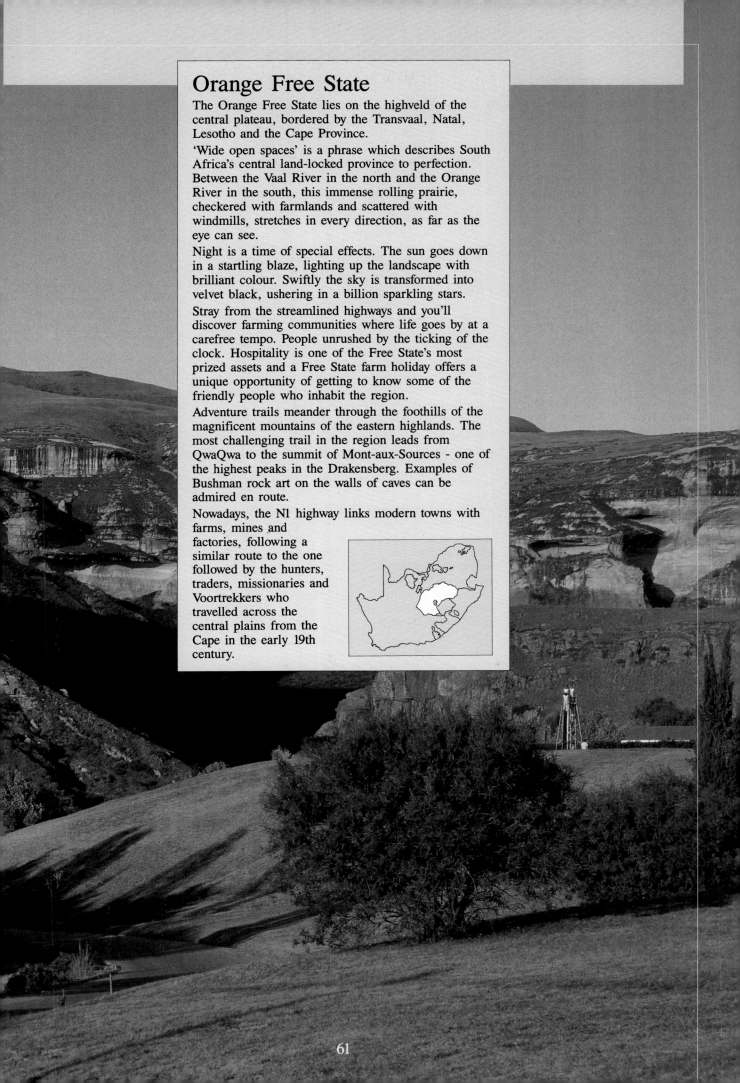

Orange Free State

The Orange Free State lies on the highveld of the central plateau, bordered by the Transvaal, Natal, Lesotho and the Cape Province.

'Wide open spaces' is a phrase which describes South Africa's central land-locked province to perfection. Between the Vaal River in the north and the Orange River in the south, this immense rolling prairie, checkered with farmlands and scattered with windmills, stretches in every direction, as far as the eye can see.

Night is a time of special effects. The sun goes down in a startling blaze, lighting up the landscape with brilliant colour. Swiftly the sky is transformed into velvet black, ushering in a billion sparkling stars.

Stray from the streamlined highways and you'll discover farming communities where life goes by at a carefree tempo. People unrushed by the ticking of the clock. Hospitality is one of the Free State's most prized assets and a Free State farm holiday offers a unique opportunity of getting to know some of the friendly people who inhabit the region.

Adventure trails meander through the foothills of the magnificent mountains of the eastern highlands. The most challenging trail in the region leads from QwaQwa to the summit of Mont-aux-Sources - one of the highest peaks in the Drakensberg. Examples of Bushman rock art on the walls of caves can be admired en route.

Nowadays, the N1 highway links modern towns with farms, mines and factories, following a similar route to the one followed by the hunters, traders, missionaries and Voortrekkers who travelled across the central plains from the Cape in the early 19th century.

Above: The National Women's Memorial: one of Bloemfontein's most striking monuments.

Below: Bloemfontein's unusual twin-spired church.

Bloemfontein

In the centre of the plains, the spring from which Bloemfontein got its name still surfaces in the middle of the city which grew around it. At one time the source of water for Bushman hunters, Sotho farmers, Voortrekkers and their oxen, today the site is occupied by a caravan park shaded by tall trees.

With its crisp highveld air, plush shopping centres, restaurants, cinemas and theatres, Bloemfontein, 'City of Roses', has all the dignity and civic pride one would expect of South Africa's judicial capital. Dominated by skyscrapers, stately historical buildings and monuments testify to its pioneering past. A striking architectural landmark, the Sand du Plessis Theatre is one of South Africa's most glamorous entertainment venues. Its repertoire includes a sumptuous choice of opera, ballet and symphony concerts.

The city is noted for its beautiful parks and gardens: the Botanical Gardens, Orchid House and Loch Logan, to mention only a few. Rose-lovers should make a point of visiting Bloemfontein in October when the annual Rose Festival is held.

And for those who enjoy delving into the past, the National Museum features outstanding anthropological exhibits, and a War Museum focuses on relics of the Anglo-Boer War.

Situated at the most central point in South Africa, the city's hotels offer a convenient stopover for motorists travelling between the Cape, Natal and the Transvaal. Bloemfontein is also an ideal base for those who wish to explore the surrounding countryside, and only 85 km from Bloemfontein, there's a fortune waiting to be won at the Thaba 'Nchu Sun casino.

Suggested Tours

Hendrik Verwoerd Dam
(Some 210 km south of Bloemfontein on the N1.)

En route to the dam, it's worth taking a detour on the R704 to the small town of Philippolis, notable for its historical buildings.

The enormous man-made lake on the Orange River (the largest in South Africa) forms part of the most extensive water supply project in southern Africa, now boosted by the Maluti Highlands Scheme further up the river in Lesotho. The dam is a major attraction for those who enjoy fishing, water-skiing, swimming and yachting. An adjacent nature reserve supports the largest springbok population in South Africa, as well as black wildebeest, red hartebeest and ostrich.

Father Claerhout's Studio
(Tweespruit, just before you reach the Thaba 'Nchu turn-off.)

The studio of the well-known artist, Fr Claerhout, is open to the public. Further information is obtainable from the Town Clerk, Tweespruit.

Thaba 'Nchu Sun Casino and Holiday Resort/Maria Moroka National Park
(Bophuthatswana, some 85 km east of Bloemfontein.)

Set at the base of the Thaba 'Nchu Mountain, the resort complex offers luxurious accommodation and standard casino facilities (blackjack, punto banco, craps, chemin de fer, American roulette and one-armed bandits). Visitors are taken on daily expeditions into the Maria Moroka National Park, in an amphitheatre formed by the Thaba 'Nchu Mountain and the Groothoek Dam. Springbok, zebra and eland are among the game species. Rangers conduct game viewing drives.

Arts and Crafts Route (in and around Clarens.)

Thirteen artists, including painters, weavers, leather workers and goldsmiths have opened their studios to the public. Further details are obtainable from the Town Clerk, Clarens.

Golden Gate Highlands National Park (300 km north-east of Bloemfontein.)

Spectacular sandstone formations characterise the region in which the park is situated. The reserve is renowned for its splendid scenery, invigorating climate and comfortable accommodation. Herds of eland, black wildebeest, blesbok, springbok and mountain reedbuck inhabit the sanctuary, also the haunt of the splendid bearded vulture and the black eagle. From the summit of Generaalskop, reached by a hiking trail, panoramic views span the surrounding area, including part of Lesotho.

In summer, the terrain is embellished with watsonias, fire lilies, red hot pokers, arum lilies and many other wild flower species. In autumn, the indigenous trees are clad in brilliant shades of red, green and yellow.

Battlefields

There are a number of Anglo-Boer War battlefields in the region. Sites are signposted. These include Paardeberg, near Jacobsdal; Roodewa, near Heilbron; Wepener, on the Lesotho border; and Jammerberg Drift on the road to East London, to mention but a few.

For further information on touring areas, restaurants, shopping centres, specialist shops and accommodation, contact your nearest SATOUR office (see back cover) or the Bloemfontein Publicity Association (see page 121).

Top: Maselspoort, on the banks of the Modder River.

Above: The city's Rose Festival is held in October every year.

Below: War Memorial: 'The Farewell'.

Left: The impressive, modern Sand du Plessis Theatre.

63

Places of Interest

A1 1 Botanical Gardens An area of 45 ha features the indigenous flora of the Free State and is divided into formal gardens, natural woodlands and wetlands. Other attractions include a lake, herbarium, orange tree arbour and tearoom.

B3 2 City Hall This well-known landmark in Bloemfontein is noted for its superb Italian marble and Burmese wood finishes.

B3 3 Civic Theatre Venue for regular opera, ballet, theatre and other productions.

B3 4 Court of Appeal Bloemfontein is the judicial capital of South Africa and as such is the home of the highest court in the land - the Appellate Division of the Supreme Court. The building is richly furnished and panelled in stinkwood.

B4 5 First Raadsaal (council chamber) Bloemfontein's oldest building, a simple thatched structure dating from 1849, was used by the Volksraad (Legislative Assembly) as its first official chambers. An adjoining building houses the Wagon Museum.

B3 6 Fountain A concrete column and city emblem in mosaic mark the site of the spring from which the city derived its name.

B3 7 Fourth Raadsaal (council chamber) This red-brick building with its domed tower and Doric columns is one of many famous landmarks in the city. It served as the last seat of assembly of the Old Republic of the Orange Free State before the British occupation of Bloemfontein in March 1900. An equestrian statue of General De Wet stands in front of the building.

C2 8 Hamilton Park The park embraces the **Orchid House** with its large collection of orchids beautifully displayed in an interior incorporating waterfalls, pools and bridges. In Union Avenue opposite the park there is a fragrance garden for the blind.

B4 9 Hertzog House The home of the famous Boer general, J B M Hertzog from 1895-1924 is now a national monument and museum.

A3 10 King's Park A rose garden containing more than 4 000 rose bushes makes this one of the prettiest parks in the 'City of Roses'. A flea market is held on the first Saturday of every month. The park also incorporates the **Zoological Gardens** where an interesting collection of birds and animals is housed, including the liger, a cross between a lion and a tiger. The zoo has one of the largest primate collections in the country.

D3 11 Maselspoort This resort, some 22 km from the city on the banks of the Modder River, features various sports and recreational facilities, in addition to accommodation, a restaurant and conference facilities.

C4 12 Military Museum Fort Bloemfontein The museum is housed in an old fort constructed in 1848 and rebuilt just before the Anglo-Boer War when it was taken over by the British. Exhibits depict the role of the South African forces during the First and Second World Wars.

B3 13 National Afrikaans Literary Museum and Research Centre Housed in the Third Raadsaal, the museum is a repository of Afrikaans literary treasures and contains manuscripts, books, photographs and personal possessions of Afrikanerdom's greatest authors. Music and theatre museums also form part of the complex and preserve musical instruments, items of theatrical interest, costumes and documentation.

B3 14 National Museum Noted for its large collection of fossils, cultural historical exhibits and archaeological displays, including the famous Florisbad skull.

B5 15 National Women's Memorial Dedicated to the more than 26,000 women and children who died in concentration camps during the Anglo-Boer War. The ashes of the Englishwoman, Emily Hobhouse, who championed the cause of the interned Boers during the war, lie buried under the monument. The adjacent **Military Museum of the Boer Republics** contains a collection of relics pertaining to the Anglo-Boer War. The research library attached to the museum houses an extensive collection of Africana and war photographs.

D1 16 Naval Hill A flat-topped hill near the city centre where British forces set up their ship's cannon during the Anglo-Boer War. **The Franklin Nature Reserve** on the slopes of the hill is a haven for eland, blesbok and springbok. The **Lamont Hussey Observatory** on the hill has been converted into a theatre.

B4 17 Old Presidency The stately Victorian building constructed in 1885 was the official residence of three presidents of the old Republic of the Orange Free State. The restored building currently houses a museum depicting the terms of office of the presidents. It is also a cultural centre for art exhibitions, theatre productions and musical events.

B1 18 Oliewenhuis Art Gallery Housed in a Neo-Cape Dutch manor house originally built to accommodate dignitaries during their visits to the city.

B3 19 Open-air Agricultural Museum Implements of different eras are displayed here together with a blacksmith's shop.

A3 20 President Swart Park Encompasses the Free State Stadium, an important sports venue, tennis courts, a heated Olympic-size pool, cricket oval, children's playground and caravan park.

C3 21 Ramblers This sports stadium has been associated with cricket since colonial times.

B3 22 Sand du Plessis Theatre An impressive modern complex where the Performing Arts Council of the Orange Free State regularly stages opera, ballet, drama, music concerts and other productions. Across the road, the H F Verwoerd Building with its massive stained glass window consisting of some 17,000 pieces of coloured glass, presents a magnificent sight when the building is lit up at night.

C3 23 Twin-spired Church With its two spires, this is one of South Africa's most distinctive churches.

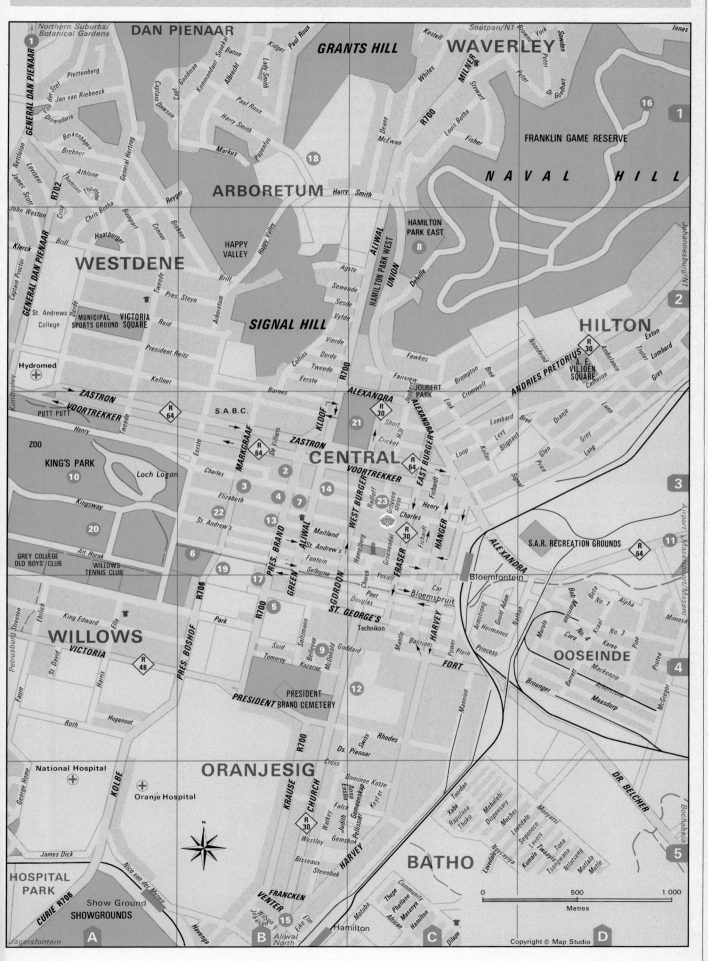

Northern Free State

When the Boers trekked away from British rule at the Cape in 1836, they crossed the Orange River and travelled north where they found vast, sparsely inhabited tracts of land. Here they outspanned their ox wagons, built homesteads, ploughed, cultivated and harvested their crops and tended cattle.

Until fairly recently, the Free State was mainly agricultural, but that changed in the 1940s with the discovery of the fabulous northern Free State goldfields. The mines produce over one third of South Africa's gold. As you approach the towns of Welkom, Odendaalsrus, Virginia and Allanridge (all built on gold), the horizon is dotted with mine dumps. Welkom was transformed from barren veld into an attractive industrial city in less than 20 years.

The scenic Willem Pretorius Game Reserve, near the town of Winburg, surrounds the Allemanskraal Dam, and supports a wide range of wildlife, including some 600 black wildebeest, reputedly the largest herd in the world. Over 900 bird species have been recorded here. The scenery is striking. Flanked by the rocky ridge of the Doringberg, it encompasses wooded gorges and open plains. The dam is stocked with indigenous fish.

On the Transvaal border, the Vaal, one of South Africa's major rivers, flows through a fertile valley lined with willow trees. Vaal Dam and Loch Vaal, two of the river's largest dams, are firm favourites among anglers and water sports enthusiasts. In summer, fun-lovers flaunting tans adorn the river banks. And when the sun goes down, fine wines and gourmet cuisine are served in plush hotels, while the rich sail by on yachts, languidly sipping their G&T's.

For holiday-makers committed to urban diversions, the larger towns have a choice of restaurants, shops and theatres.

Above: Solitude and silence on the lazy waters of the Vaal.

Below: Statue of the great Voortrekker leader, Sarel Cilliers, at Kroonstad.

Above: Masses of cannas enhance the landscape of the north-eastern Free State.

Below: When the Boers trekked from the Cape to the Orange Free State, they found vast tracts of arable land.

Left: *An enormous herd of wildebeest roams free in the Willem Pretorius Game Reserve.*

Below: *Welkom was transformed from barren veld into an attractive city in less than 20 years.*

Above: *The Vals River offers wonderful opportunities for a wide range of water sports.*

Right: *Nature reserves support a great diversity of bird life.*

Below: *The climate lends itself to an outdoor life style.*

Below: *Springbok inhabit most of the Free State's game reserves.*

Places of Interest

C3 1 Bethlehem Situated in the famous maize triangle, Bethlehem features beautiful historic sandstone buildings and excellent facilities for tourists. The **Pretoriuskloof Nature Reserve** in the centre of the town nestles between perpendicular cliffs along the Jordan River and supports a variety of wild birds and small mammals. **Loch Athlone Resort,** on the southern outskirts of the town, offers accommodation, various amenities and opportunities for water sports. Hiking trails can be undertaken in the vicinity of the town.

A2 2 Bloemhof Dam Situated just below the confluence of the Vaal and Vet Rivers and bounded in the north by the **Bloemhof Dam Nature Reserve.** The reserve is home to a variety of game, including white rhino, but is especially noted for its excellent fishing potential. The peninsula between the two arms of the dam comprises the **Sandveld Nature Reserve.** A great many bird species occur here and there are facilities for camping and caravanning. Hunting is permitted in both reserves in winter.

B3 3 Erfenis Dam Nature Reserve On the banks of the **Erfenis Dam** where boating and angling are popular. Waterfowl are a speciality here, particularly African shelduck and Egyptian geese. Various species of game including the unusual white springbok and yellow blesbok may also be seen. Camping and caravanning are permitted.

D3 4 Harrismith Starting point of the scenic **Highlands Route** through the eastern Free State. The town serves a thriving agricultural community. The **Drakensberg Botanical Gardens** are noted for their variety of indigenous flora and feature various trails, one of which leads to a blockhouse built by the British during the Anglo-Boer War. The **Town Hall,** built in 1907, is a typical example of the sandstone architecture of the time. A petrified tree trunk next to the hall is estimated to be 150 million years old. The Berg Marathon up the Platberg, held in October annually, is one of the sports highlights of the year. The tradition goes back to the Anglo-Boer War when a British soldier, Major Belcher, accepted a challenge to run to the summit in 60 minutes.

B2 5 Kroonstad Situated on the Vals River, the town offers many opportunities for water sports. The holiday resort **Kroonpark** is a popular inland resort. The town boasts fine sandstone buildings, including the old town hall, the old market square post office and a Dutch Reformed Church. **St Patrick's Cathedral** is renowned as a repository of South African modern art. A one-day hiking trail just outside the town enables one to appreciate the many species of birds and fine examples of Bushman paintings which occur in the area. The **Mealie Route** in the district makes an interesting outing. It includes a visit to a maize farm, rosefarm, rose nursery and pottery studio.

B1 6 Loch Vaal The Vaal River was backed up against a concrete barrage here in 1923, providing not only for the requirements of cities and industries in the area, but also for man's recreational needs.

D3 7 Mount Everest Game Reserve The reserve provides sanctuary for a number of game species. Game viewing in open vehicles, several hiking trails and accommodation are available.

B1 8 Parys A town scenically situated on the banks of the Vaal River and much appreciated by water sports fans. Various picnic spots, resorts and facilities are found along the river and on the islands in the river. One island features a golf course which is accessible only via a suspension bridge.

C1 9 Sasolburg A modern industrial town where coal is converted to oil, from which petrol is refined. The **Highveld Gardens** feature many indigenous plants and a bird park. A holiday resort on the banks of the Vaal River offers accommodation and a variety of recreational facilities. The adjacent skating rink is reputedly the biggest in the southern hemisphere.

A3 10 Theunissen district This rich maize area yields an unexpected product: wine, which is produced and sold on one of the farms north of Theunissen. Wine tastings and cellar tours are available. The farm also boasts a fine collection of cycads and a cycad nursery.

C1 11 Vaal Dam Often referred to as the highveld's inland sea, this vast expanse of water covers some 300 square kilometres. It serves as Johannesburg's principal source of water and is a popular water sports venue. Numerous resorts line the shoreline. The **Vaal Dam Nature Reserve** on the northern bank has typical highveld vegetation. The dam supports barbel, carp and yellowfish and attracts many bird species, including yellow-billed duck, coot, great white egret, Egyptian goose and fish eagle.

C2 12 Vegkop Battlefield The site of a battle between the Voortrekkers and the Matabele army of Mzilikazi in 1836. The area features the ruins of corbelled houses of the Leghoya people who settled in this area in the early 17th century.

B2 13 Virginia Founded after the gold discoveries of the 1940s. Visits to gold mines in the area can be arranged and displays of tribal dancing can often be seen on these visits. The Sand River which flows through the town provides opportunities for water sports. A holiday resort and a caravan park along the river provide various amenities. There is also a small game park which accommodates mainly the smaller antelope species.

B2 14 Welkom Centre of the Free State goldfields, but despite its industrial nature a beautifully tranquil city with many lovely parks and green belts. The various mine evaporation dams and pans on the outskirts of the city attract a prolific bird life including flocks of pink flamingoes and even a large seagull population. Visits to gold mines may be arranged through the Publicity Association.

B3 15 Willem Pretorius Game Reserve This reserve incorporates the Allemanskraal Dam and accommodates a variety of game, including white rhino and buffalo. A public resort overlooking the dam offers self-catering accommodation, a restaurant and facilities for various sports such as tennis, bowls and golf. Walking trails may be undertaken.

B3 16 Winburg Steeped in Voortrekker history and at the height of the Great Trek, capital of the Republic Trans-Oranje. The **Voortrekker Museum** and various monuments reflect the history of the region.

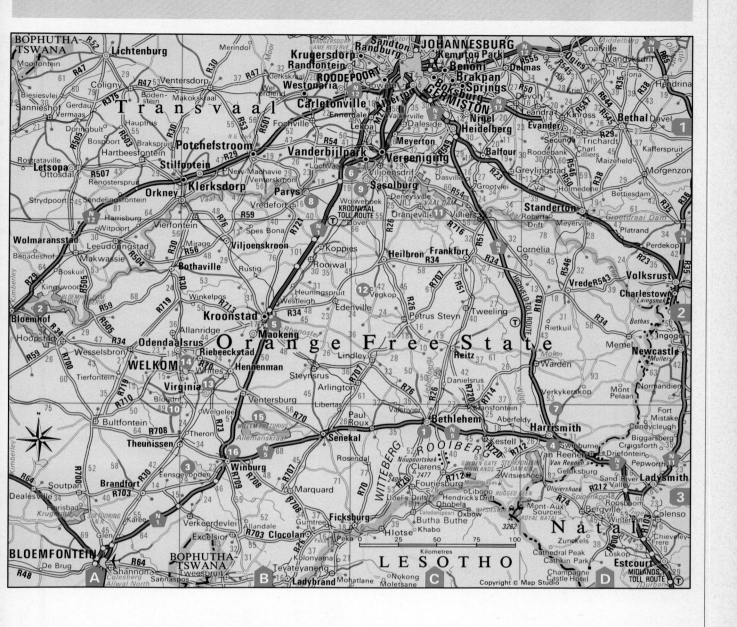

Southern Free State

Travellers often experience a sense of excitement when crossing the Orange River from the Cape Province, and discovering on the northern bank a different, more fertile world than the one just left behind. The region has a fascination all of its own: grassy plains quilted with farmlands, isolated mountains and rocky hillocks. Scattered towns serve agricultural communities quietly going about their rural activities.

Pride and joy of the Free State, the eastern highlands are best explored by following the Highland Route. In spring, the cool sparkling air is filled with the scent of flowers, cherry blossoms and herbs; summer is a time of ripening harvests and in winter, the cliffs are shrouded with snow.

The Golden Gate Highlands National Park is a tremendous holiday drawcard because of its superlative scenery, invigorating climate and comfortable accommodation. The park derives its name from the brilliant, blazing shades of gold cast by the sun on the region's imposing sandstone cliffs. The park is home to herds of springbok, eland, red hartebeest and an abundant bird life, including the rare black eagle and the lammergeyer. Clear mountain streams stocked with trout attract appreciative fishermen.

The long lazy flow of the river from which the province derives its name is especially popular among holiday-makers. The river is also the site of one of the country's most astounding engineering feats: the Hendrik Verwoerd Dam - an enormous inland sea. Its expanse of water and the pleasant resort on its banks provide a relaxing interlude in the journey across the Karoo. The dam is a major attraction for those who enjoy swimming, water-skiing, fishing and yachting.

Above: *Farmlands planted with maize stretch from one horizon to another.*

Right: *Cinderella Castle, in Clarens, was built with thousands of beer bottles.*

Below: *Cosmos flowers splash the autumn countryside with colour.*

Top: *Voortrekker Memorial, near Winburg.*

Above: *QwaQwa is renowned for its decorative hand-woven carpets.*

Below: *A black eagle surveys the fertile Free State plains.*

Above: *A relaxing travel option between Bethlehem and Ficksburg.*

Left: *Spectacular scenery is the main feature of the Golden Gate Highlands National Park.*

Below left: *'Wide open spaces' describes the province to perfection.*

Above: *The Orange River lily - one of the fairest flowers of the veld.*

Left: *Holiday resort, Hendrik Verwoerd Dam.*

Places of Interest

B3 1 Bethulie A farming and railway centre off the main highway, but with interesting tourist attractions. The **Pellissier House Museum,** housed in what is thought to be the oldest settler-built structure north of the Orange, reflects the history of the district. The **D H Steyn Bridge** over the Orange River on the outskirts of the town is at 2,993 m the longest bridge in the country. The **Bethulie Dam** offers water sports and angling and the adjoining **Mynhardt Game Reserve,** accommodation and game viewing.

D1 2 Clarens A picturesque town situated in a mountain basin with wonderful views of the Maluti Mountains. An unusual man-made attraction is **Cinderella Castle,** built out of more than 55,000 beer bottles. Artists and craftsmen of the district regularly exhibit at craft markets on the town square and in the Twin Oaks and Guinea-Feather Galleries.

C1 3 Clocolan Another good base from which the scenic eastern highlands may be explored. Two dams in the area offer excellent angling opportunities.

C1 4 Ficksburg Situated at the centre of an important cherry and asparagus-producing area. Particularly beautiful in spring when the cherry blossoms bloom. The annual Cherry Festival is a highlight on the local calendar. Farms in the district provide accommodation. At the **Hoekfontein Game Farm** game viewing is offered in an open landrover. Accommodation is available. Hiking may be enjoyed on the farm.

D1 5 Fouriesburg An attractive caravan park on the outskirts of the village is the starting and end point of the five-day **Brandwater Hiking Trail.** The 65-km trail leads past magnificent sandstone formations in the district. Three of the overnight shelters are in caves, and one of them, **Salpeterkrans,** is reputed to be one of the largest sandstone caves in the southern hemisphere. Holiday farms in the area provide comfortable accommodation and recreational facilities.

D1 6 Golden Gate Highlands National Park
Spectacular mountain scenery is the main feature of this reserve and many walks and trails enable one to enjoy this to the full. Game viewing and bird-watching are also popular pursuits. More than 100 bird species occur and these include the rare bearded vulture (lammergeyer), black eagle, Cape vulture and other raptors. Accommodation is available in two camps and a caravan park.

A3 7 Hendrik Verwoerd Dam Covering some 374 square kilometres and with a storage capacity of 5,958 million cubic metres, this dam forms part of the Orange River Development Scheme. The water is used for extensive irrigation schemes and the production of hydro-electrical power. In terms of recreation the dam is a popular venue for water sports. **The Hendrik Verwoerd Dam Nature Reserve** on the northern banks accommodates the largest springbok population in the country as well as other game. A public resort on the western bank has accommodation, tennis courts, a pool, golf course and various other amenities.

C2 8 Ladybrand A historic town close to the border post between South Africa and Lesotho with many picturesque sandstone buildings. **The Catharina Brand Museum** has many fine exhibits, notably a variety of Bushman artefacts found in the district and copies of rock paintings. Also of interest are the **Rose Cottage Cave** in the district which is an important archaeological site and the **Modderpoort Cave Church** which has been in use since 1869. A holiday resort close by affords opportunities to explore the scenic countryside either on foot or on horseback.

A3 9 P K le Roux Dam The second largest dam in the country; part of the Orange River Development Scheme. The **Doornkloof** and **Rolfontein Nature Reserves** on the Cape Province side of the dam provide sanctuary for various game and bird species. Hiking trails are available.

A3 10 Philippolis Dating from 1823, Philippolis was one of the first towns established in the Free State. Many of the old buildings have been declared national monuments. These include the Dutch Reformed Church, the library building and some of the quaint houses built in the Karoo style. The **Transgariep** and **Delta Museums** depict the history of the region.

D1 11 Phuthaditjhaba Capital of the mountain world of QwaQwa. Items such as mohair wall-hangings, karakul carpets, hand-painted porcelain, copper and brass work, baskets, cane furniture and glassware are manufactured and sold in the industrial centre on the outskirts of the town.

B3 12 Smithfield The third oldest town in the Free State. Of interest are the **Caledon River Museum** in town and the **Carmel** and **Beersheba** mission stations in the district. The two-day **Stokstert Hiking Trail** traverses the region. A farm holiday may be enjoyed on one of the farms on the banks of the Caledon River.

B1 13 Soetdoring Nature Reserve A sanctuary for lion, cheetah, brown hyena and several species of antelope.

D1 14 Sterkfontein Dam Nature Reserve Situated in the foothills of the Drakensberg on the banks of the Sterkfontein Dam, the reserve offers water sports, angling and bird-watching. Chalets and a camping site are available.

B3 15 Tussen-die-Riviere Nature Reserve
Wedged between the Orange and the Caledon Rivers, the reserve offers game viewing in summer and hunting in winter. Game includes eland, kudu, gemsbok, zebra and white rhino. Accommodation is available.

C2 16 Wepener Close to the Lesotho border. Serves a wool, grain, corn and livestock-farming area. The town features many examples of the sandstone architecture of the southern Free State. The **Welbedacht Dam** nearby offers angling and boating.

D1 17 Wolhuterskop Nature Reserve Home to a variety of game and bird species. Visit the historic sandstone homestead of the first owners of the farm, Gerrand Dam, and a dense pine forest where one hears the cooing of hundreds of turtledoves.

C3 18 Zastron Situated at the foot of the Aasvoëlberg which features the famous **Eye of Zastron,** a hole nine metres in diameter through the sandstone cliff. Fine examples of Bushman rock art occur on various farms in the district.

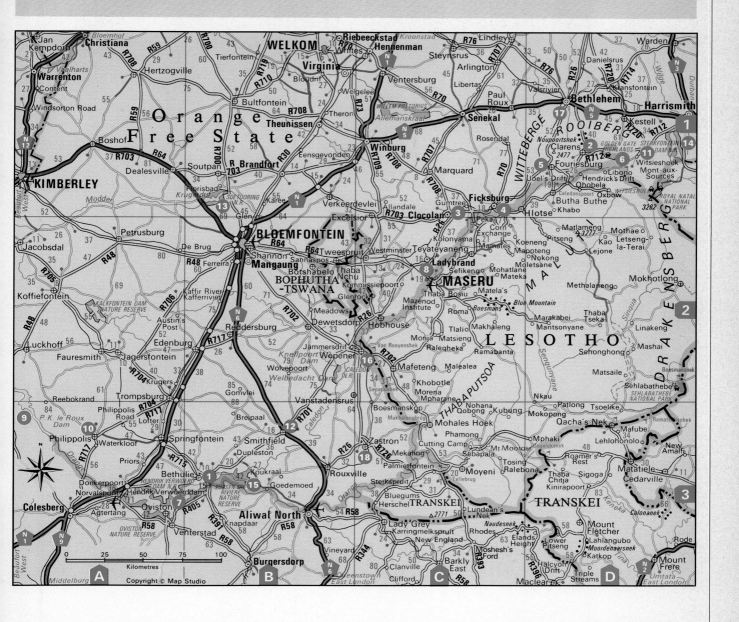

Cape Province

The Cape Province is bounded by Namibia, Botswana, the Orange Free State, Lesotho, Ciskei and Transkei, the Indian Ocean in the east and the Atlantic in the west.

Not surprisingly, South Africa's largest province experiences a phenomenal climatic, geographic and scenic spectrum: a coastline in places rugged, elsewhere placid; soaring mountains and tumbling rivers; a vast semi-desert which blooms in spring; tall forests and a glorious floral kingdom.

In the winter rainfall 'Mediterranean' region of the western Cape, every season has its own enchantment: the flowers of spring, the ripening orchards of summer, the reds and golds of autumn, the cool freshness of winter. In stark contrast, the arid Richtersveld, in the north-west, features rocky outcrops, space, silence and a spartan vegetation.

The lakes, mountains and forests of the Garden Route are bordered by impressive mountain ranges, and the interior is reached via a number of magnificent passes. The Little Karoo features undulating hills and fertile valleys, while the Great Karoo is a thirstland dotted with isolated farms.

Pristine beaches and tiny fishing resorts occur from Port Nolloth in the north-west to Morgan's Bay, south of the Transkei border. The coastline is acclaimed for its broad, sandy beaches punctuated by rocky promontories, coves, river mouths and lagoons.

From the wild Agulhas coast at the southernmost tip of Africa to the glory of Namaqualand in bloom, this is a province of extraordinary beauty and variety. A paradise for sightseers, historians, naturalists, surfers, fishermen and mountain climbers.

Cape Peninsula

When Jan van Riebeeck arrived at the Cape in 1652, the territory was occupied solely by nomadic Hottentots and Bushmen, eking out a living from the land. Since then, visitors to the Cape Peninsula have enthused about its mountains and fertile valleys, its abundant indigenous flora and its sweeping beaches.

Both coastlines of the peninsula have beaches with dazzling white sand. Among more than 100 to choose from, Muizenberg and St James have multicoloured changing booths; Clifton attracts the bikini brigade. People-watchers stroll on the Sea Point Promenade, and nudists bare all at Sandy Bay. The charming village of Kalk Bay features brightly coloured trawlers and weather-beaten fishermen.

The best view of the city - and beyond - is from the top of Table Mountain. Chapman's Peak Drive provides another unforgettable scenic experience. The 10-km road offers a series of panoramas across Chapman's Bay to Hout Bay Harbour, alive with the bustle of fishing fleets.

A popular drive runs from Simon's Town through the Cape of Good Hope Nature Reserve to Cape Point. The reserve is the Cape's largest natural wild flower garden, particularly lovely in spring. On a clear day, from the Cape Point lookout platform, the view stretches to distant horizons, beyond False Bay and Cape Hangklip.

The peninsula, which forms part of the Cape Floral Kingdom, has more indigenous plant species per square metre than anywhere else on earth: among them, proteas, ericas, lilies, irises and orchids. Within easy driving distance from Cape Town, nature reserves, game parks and bird sanctuaries attract those who appreciate wildlife in all its many forms.

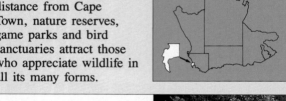

Top: Mostert's Mill, impeccably restored, was built in 1796.

Above: From Table Mountain, the views are spectacular.

Right: Kirstenbosch National Botanic Gardens, Constantia.

Below: Hout Bay, alive with the bustle of fishing fleets.

Left: Chapman's Peak Drive — a scenic masterpiece.

Above and right: The region is renowned for the diversity of its bird life.

Below left: Fun in the sun for the younger set at Muizenberg.

Below: Fish Hoek beach: a popular catamaran launching pad.

Above: The Peninsula alone has over 100 erica species.

Left: Sunworshippers gravitate to Clifton's beautiful beaches.

Places of Interest

B4 1 Cape of Good Hope Nature Reserve Extending along 40 km of coastline, this fynbos-rich plateau accommodates a variety of antelope and an abundant bird life. There are several beaches and good angling spots along the coastline. The reserve also has a restaurant, gift shop and small museum.

A3 2 Chapman's Peak Drive In addition to wonderful views, the drive provides access to excellent rock climbs and mountain walks.

C2 3 D F Malan Airport A bus service operates between the airport and the terminal in Adderley Street.

B3 4 Fish Hoek One of the many popular seaside resorts along the peninsula with a fine safe bathing beach. A stipulation by Lord Charles Somerset in the original grant of the land that no public house be kept on the farm has been strictly adhered to. The sale of liquor is prohibited in Fish Hoek.

B1 5 Green Point Lighthouse Dating from 1824, this is the oldest lighthouse in the country. Visits may be arranged through the lighthouse keeper.

B2 6 Groot Constantia The oldest wine-making centre in South Africa is now a State-owned experimental wine farm and the homestead on the estate, granted to early Cape governor Van der Stel in 1685, a museum. Furnished with antiques and old paintings, the manor house is an elegant reminder of a more gracious age. The wine museum in the cellar is of particular interest. Wine may be purchased on the estate. There are two restaurants on the estate.

B2 7 Groote Schuur Estate Situated on the slopes of Devil's Peak above the University of Cape Town, the estate was bequeathed to the nation by Cecil John Rhodes, prime minister of the Cape from 1890 to 1896. An impressive Doric style temple commemorates the statesman. The tearoom/restaurant above the memorial is open daily. A herd of free-running fallow deer roam the surrounding forest.

A2 8 Hout Bay This picturesque village with a large fishing harbour is the centre of the snoek industry and headquarters of the crayfishing fleet. **Mariner's Wharf,** on the quay, is a unique seafood emporium featuring a fresh fish and Cape rock lobster market, gift shop, restaurant and take-away outlets. Visitors will also enjoy the harbour, the museum, **World of Birds** where over 3,000 birds (450 species) can be viewed and launch trips to **Seal Island.**

B2 9 Irma Stern Museum The home of this internationally known artist is now a museum where not only her own work, but also Congolese masks, oriental ceramics, old furniture and other items collected on her travels are displayed.

B2 10 Josephine Mill Situated on the banks of the Liesbeek River, this mill dating from 1818 is still in perfect working condition. The **Rugby Museum** on the first floor of the mill building will delight rugby fans.

B2 11 Mostert's Mill This wind-operated mill dating from 1796 is the only Dutch windmill in the Cape still in working order.

B3 12 Muizenberg Cradled between the sea and high mountains, this famous seaside resort boasts a magnificent 35-km stretch of beach and a relatively warm surf. Places of interest include **De Post Huys,** a lookout post and signal station from the early settlement days, and the cottage in which Cecil Rhodes died, which is now maintained as a museum. The **Natale Labia Museum** contains fine furniture and works of art. The **Rondevlei Bird Sanctuary** is home to over 200 species of birds.

B2 13 National Botanic Gardens of Kirstenbosch Sprawled over 560 ha on the eastern slopes of Table Mountain, the gardens contain 4,000 species of indigenous plants of which 2,600 are endemic to the Cape Peninsula. Plants include proteas, heaths, gladioli, watsonias and Namaqualand daisies. Although beautiful and colourful throughout the year, spring is undoubtedly the best season to visit. The offices of the Botanical Society of South Africa, the Compton Herbarium and a restaurant/tearoom are situated in the grounds.

B1 14 Observatory South Africa's first observatory, established in 1821. Since the establishment of the South African Astronomical Observatory at Sutherland in the Karoo, Cape Town's observatory has been used by amateur astronomers only.

A1 15 Sea Point A densely populated residential area featuring a cosmopolitan mixture of modern skyscrapers and Victorian buildings above a rock-strewn shore dotted with small beaches. Sea Point has a three-kilometre long promenade and a great concentration of hotels, restaurants and night clubs.

B3 16 Silvermine Nature Reserve This reserve on a high plateau in the Steenberg Mountains is a fine example of the Cape mountain flora and one of the peninsula's most picturesque picnic spots. It is reached via the Old Cape Way (M64) which offers wonderful views over False Bay and the peninsula's lakes.

B4 17 Simon's Town Headquarters of the South African Navy, the town's naval associations go back to the time of the British occupation of the Cape when it was the base for their South African squadron. Many interesting buildings, particularly in St George's Street, reflect the history of the town. **Admiralty House** built in 1740, the **Martello Tower** which houses the South African Naval Museum, and the **Residency Museum** depicting the history of the town, are among them.

B2 18 Wynberg Cape Town's largest suburb, featuring many restored cottages and antique shops. The area known as Wynberg Village in Victoria and Durban Roads has been preserved and comprises many pre-1850 houses and buildings. Maynardville has an open-air theatre known for its Shakespearean productions.

C3 19 Zeekoevlei and Sandvlei Two of several small lakes off False Bay. Popular water sports venues, they have caravan parks.

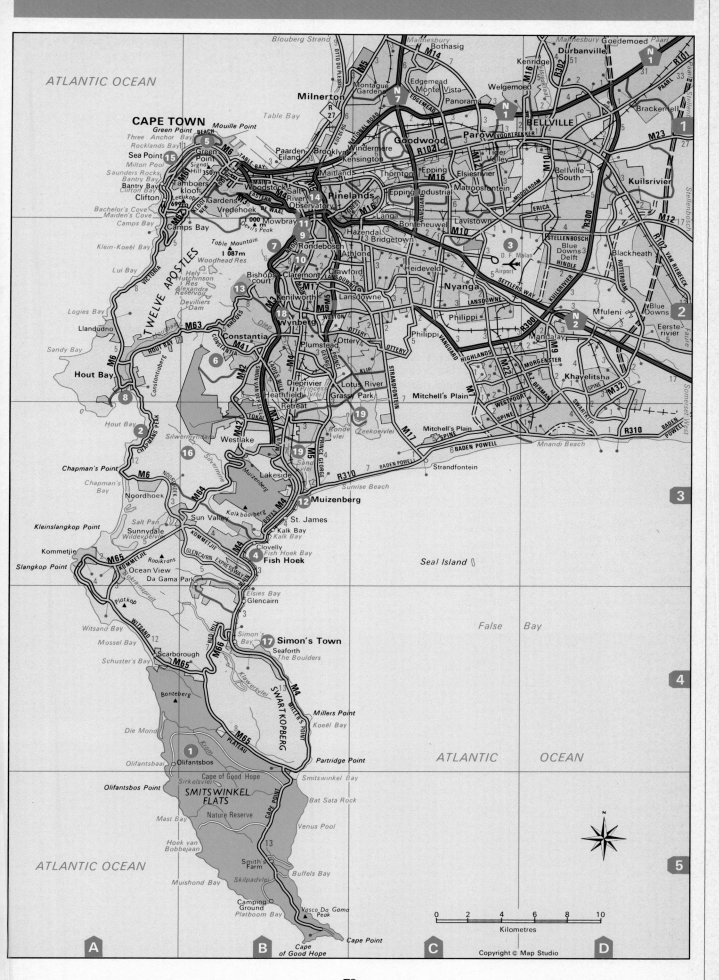

Cape Town

In 1652 Jan van Riebeeck sailed into Table Bay and laid the foundations of South Africa's oldest city. His first undertaking was to establish a vegetable garden for the purpose of providing passing merchant ships with fresh food. Before long, weary sailors from around the world dropped anchor in the bay to replenish supplies. The settlement soon earned the title: 'Tavern of the Seas', and to this day, Cape Town has maintained a reputation for friendly hospitality.

With its majestic Table Mountain backdrop, Cape Town is one of the most beautiful cities in the world. An eclectic mix of architectural styles reflects the tastes and dictates of the past - and the more functional demands of the 20th century. The city's Edwardian and Victorian buildings have been meticulously preserved, and many outstanding examples of Cape Dutch architecture are found in the city and its environs.

Cobblestoned streets, mosques and the flat-roofed pastel homes of the Malay Quarter enhance a cosmopolitan ambience, and in a recent development, the restoration of the Victoria and Alfred Waterfront evokes images of the seafaring activities of the 19th century. For a closer look at life at the Cape in earlier times, interesting historical collections are on display in several museums.

Cape Town's shopping options invite you to endlessly browse - and buy. Elegant shopping malls, department stores, antique shops and art galleries abound. Specialist boutiques in Long Street and the narrow little alleys intersecting it offer an enticing array of unusual articles not readily obtainable elsewhere.

At the end of the day, gourmets and lovers of sophisticated entertainment have a treat in store.

Top: *Cape Town also has an ultra-modern aspect.*

Above: *The South African Museum, off Government Avenue.*

Below: *For exceptional views, take a ride in the cable car.*

Suggested Tours

The following scheduled tours depart on a regular basis from Cape Town:

City Tour

Cape Town by Night

Cape Peninsula

Table Mountain/
Cape Point

Table Mountain/
Bloubergstrand

Wine Routes

Historical Buildings Route (walking tour)

Namaqualand Spring Flower Route

Whale Route

Hermanus

West Coast

Visitors with transport have the advantage of flexibility and a great many additional options, including the following:

Cape Arts and Crafts Route

Outlets are based in the region which stretches from Simon's

Left: The Victoria & Alfred Waterfront evokes images of early nautical activities.

Below: Cape Town's shops invite you to browse — and buy.

Town to Cape Town, and from Stellenbosch to Clanwilliam. They offer merchandise ranging from ethnic creations, toys, ceramics and jewellery to work produced by talented South African artists. Visitors have the opportunity of admiring, buying and meeting the artists. Maps giving addresses and telephone numbers of galleries and shops are available from **SATOUR** and **CAPTOUR.** Symbols indicate the specialities of each outlet.

Cape Antique Route

Some of the best antique dealers in the country are participating members of the Cape Antique Route, encompassing the peninsula, Paarl, Franschhoek and Stellenbosch. A brochure, obtainable from **SATOUR** and **CAPTOUR,** provides maps, information on the various towns, and historical details pertaining to the relevant periods.

Four Passes Scenic Route

A circular route of roughly 230 km may be followed by crossing the Boland Mountains over the Helshoogte, Franschhoek, Viljoen's and Sir Lowry's Passes. Start with the Helshoogte Pass, and drive through woodlands, winelands and orchards, past estates of the Stellenbosch Wine Route (lunch at Boschendal is highly recommended), the Rhodes fruit farms, some farms of the Franschhoek Wine Route, the Huguenot Monument and Grabouw (the heart of apple-growing country). From the summit of Sir Lowry's Pass, the views encompass False Bay and Table Mountain. Return to Cape Town via the tranquil seaside resorts of Gordon's Bay and Strand.

Left: One of the world's most photogenic views.

Ceres Fruit Route

This scenic route links the towns of Grabouw, Tulbagh and Wolseley. On the way, you can visit museums, craft shops, farms, farm stalls and co-ops, follow mountain trails and sample apples, pears, apricots, nectarines, plums, peaches and grapes.

Both routes can be completed in a few hours or you can make a day - or more - of it, following detours, stopping for lunch and sightseeing, and spending the night at hospitable country inns.

For further information on tours, details of tour operators, restaurants, shopping centres, specialist shops and accommodation, contact your nearest SATOUR office (see back cover) or CAPTOUR (see page 121).

Above: High-spirited minstrels are a traditional ingredient of the annual Cape Festival.

Below: A familiar sight in the city centre.

Places of Interest

B4 1 Bertram House Museum This brick Georgian townhouse has been restored to its 1820 Regency splendour complete with authentic furnishing.

B3 2 Bo-Kaap Bounded by Rose, Wale, Chiappini and Shortmarket Streets, the area has many mosques and is notable for the distinctive style of house favoured by the descendants of the Malay slaves brought to the Cape during the Dutch occupation. The **Bo-Kaap Museum** depicts the historic way of life of the city's Muslim community.

D3 3 Castle of Good Hope Dating from 1666, the castle is one of the oldest European structures in South Africa. Guided tours take in torture chambers, cells with ancient graffiti, the bulk of the William Fehr Collection of Africana, a military museum and a maritime museum.

C3 4 City Hall and Grand Parade Built in 1905, the city hall is a blend of Italian Renaissance and British colonial styles and forms a dignified background to the bustle of the Grand Parade where flea markets are held on Wednesdays and Saturdays and flowers are sold daily. Symphony concerts are held in the city hall on Thursdays and Sundays.

C3 5 Company's Garden A botanical garden containing indigenous and exotic plants on the site of the original vegetable garden established by the Dutch East India Company. The oak-lined **Government Avenue** leads through the garden.

C3 6 Cultural History Museum Housed in a former slave lodge of the Dutch East India Company, the museum contains the cultural and Africana sections of the South African Museum. Highlights are the stamp, coin and gun collections and the 19th century pharmacy.

C3 7 Greenmarket Square This cobbled square with shady trees derived its name from the market gardeners who used to sell their wares here in previous centuries. A flea market is held daily, weather permitting.

C3 8 Groote Kerk This historic church completed in 1704 is the oldest in the country. It houses beautiful collections of Cape silver, old family crests and a handcarved wooden pulpit by Anton Anreith.

C3 9 Houses of Parliament The impressive building is the seat of the legislative government of South Africa. It also houses a parliamentary museum containing works of art and other memorabilia dating back to the first Cape Parliament of 1854.

C4 10 Jewish Museum Housed in South Africa's oldest synagogue, the museum has a collection of Jewish ceremonial art and displays tracing the history of Jewish communities in the Cape.

C3 11 Koopmans de Wet House This double-storey 18th century town house with its elegant façade displays a priceless collection of Cape Dutch furniture, paintings and other antiques.

B3 12 Long Street Victorian buildings complete with wrought-iron tracery and turrets line the upper section of the street which is renowned for its second-hand bookshops.

D3 13 Nico Malan Opera House and Theatre Home of the Cape Performing Arts Board where regular performances of opera, ballet, drama and music are staged.

C3 14 Old Town House Built in 1755 to accommodate the Town Guard, the building now houses the Michaelis Collection of 17th century Dutch and Flemish oil paintings.

C4 15 Rust en Vreugd A restored 200-year old double-storey town house containing part of the William Fehr Collection of watercolours, lithographs and engravings by early South African artists.

C3 16 Sendinggestig Museum Housed in a restored Dutch Reformed mission church dating from 1802.

C3 17 South African Association of Arts Venue for exhibitions of contemporary South African art.

B4 18 South African Museum The oldest museum in the country has extensive natural history collections of mammals, reptiles, birds, fish and insects. The whale gallery, life-sized models of Bushmen and examples of their paintings are of particular interest. A planetarium forms part of the complex.

C4 19 South African National Gallery Contains a permanent exhibition of local and international art. The collection of 18th and 19th century British sporting pictures is exceptional.

C3 20 South African Public Library A national reference and research library with some 400,000 books and a vast collection of Africana.

D2 21 Table Bay Harbour The second largest harbour in the country; handles passenger liners and cargo ships.

A5 22 Table Mountain This familiar landmark may be explored either on foot along one of the many pathways or by cable car from the Lower Cable Station in Table Mountain Road, Kloofnek. The view from the top of the mountain is spectacular and the restaurant there a good place from which to enjoy it.

C3 23 Trafalgar Place Flower Market A colourful display of flowers and heaths await those who wish to admire or to buy.

C4 24 Tuynhuys An impressive mansion which was once the alternative residence of the State President and now serves as his offices.

C1 25 Victoria & Alfred Waterfront The recently converted waterfront is a working harbour and lively entertainment area. In addition to historical buildings, a hotel in the restored 1904 north quay warehouse, restaurants, a theatre and speciality shops, other attractions are the **South African Maritime Museum** and a waterfront brewery. Waterfront walks, tours, helicopter flips and boat trips on a historic steam tug, a wooden work boat and the Penny Ferry are also available.

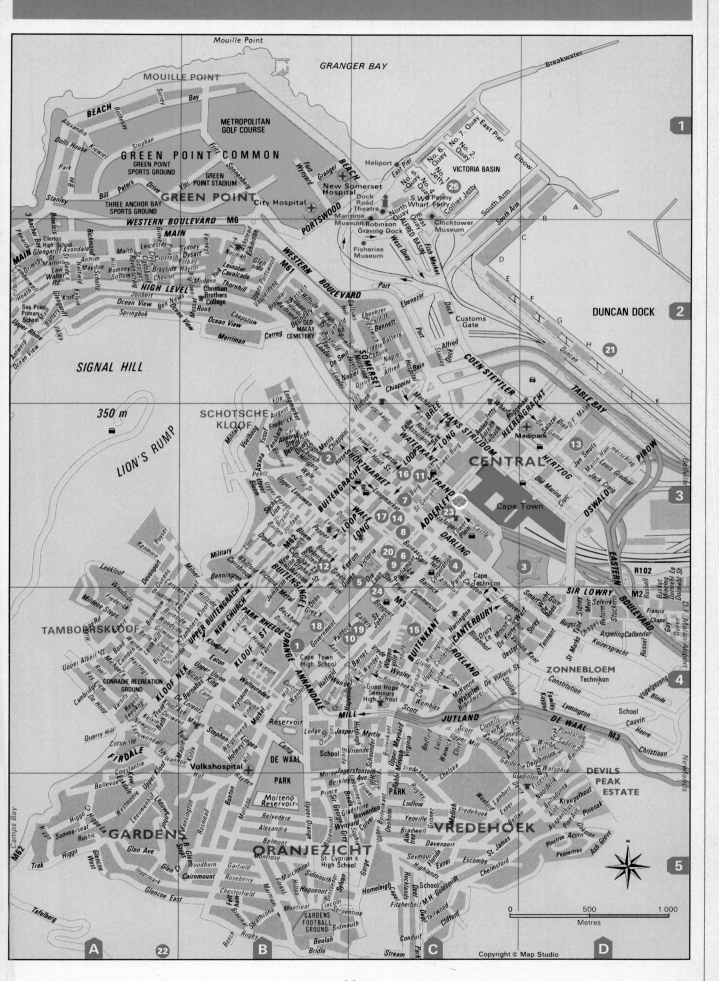

South-western Cape

Skeletons of ships testify to the periodic violence of the waves at the place where two oceans meet. In calmer mood, the coast provides ideal conditions for anglers: silence, solitude and countless varieties and numbers of fish.

The deep blue waters of the Atlantic yield a lavish harvest of mussels, oysters and crayfish, and within a 50-km radius of Saldanha, there is some of the finest line fishing in the world. Good news for bird watchers! Huge shoals of fish inhabit the west coast waters, attracting a regular following of cormorants, Cape gannets, flamingoes and pelicans.

Scattered along the southern Cape coast, fashionable seaside resorts abound. Among them, Hermanus, dubbed 'the Riviera of South Africa', demands a pause, even if you only have time for a stroll on the seafront to ogle the views and the palatial holiday homes of the upper crust.

Struisbaai, Gansbaai and Pearly Beach appeal especially to outdoor people who enjoy an unstructured holiday agenda, with fishing, swimming and hiking as priorities. At Arniston, restored fishermen's cottages provide inspiration for artists and photographers.

Dominated by indigo mountains, the Cape Wine Routes are immensely popular throughout the year. Major estates within easy reach of Cape Town are situated in the Stellenbosch, Paarl and Franschhoek districts. The winelands provide wonderful opportunities for wine lovers to sample and buy noble vintages, to explore exquisitely furnished Cape Dutch manor houses and to delve into the history of the area.

From Paarl, it's a short and pleasant drive into the wine and fruit-producing regions of the Breede River Valley where picturesque little towns, country walks and mountain trails provide endless scope for exploration.

Top: *La Dauphine — an elegant example of Cape Dutch architecture.*

Above: *The wines of the western Cape are renowned worldwide.*

Below: *Harvest-time in the winelands.*

Right: *Craggy mountains overlook the Hex River Valley.*

Left: The charming sanderling frequents semi-deserted beaches.

Right: Grootbaai: a premier venue for boardsailing contests.

Below right: Restored fishermen's cottages, Waenhuiskrans.

Below left: The Jonkershoek Valley — a scenic paradise.

Below: Approach to the Huguenot Tunnel from Worcester.

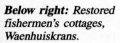

Left: Oom Samie se Winkel, an old trading store in Stellenbosch.

Below left: 'Happy Hour' at the Lord Milner in Matjiesfontein.

Below: The delicate pink cliff lily blooms in autumn.

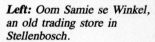

Places of Interest

B3 1 Betty's Bay Popular among fishermen and nature lovers. The **Harold Porter Botanic Garden** is renowned for its wild flowers, particularly the rare disa. The only penguin reserve on the mainland is situated in Betty's Bay.

A2 2 Bloubergstrand Holiday resort with spectacular view of Table Mountain and Cape Town. Fishing is good, as is surfing and swimming, despite the cold surf. Wild flowers abound in spring.

D3 3 Bredasdorp Situated in a prosperous wool and grain-farming district. The local museum is thought to be the only shipwreck museum in the world and houses fascinating relics. The **Bredasdorp Nature Reserve** preserves the fynbos of the area, including proteas and ericas.

C2 4 Caledon The town which today is the centre of a wheat and sheep-farming area, developed as result of the hot springs there. A hotel at the springs provides accommodation and other amenities. The **Caledon Museum** with its many Victorian antiques and the **Venster Kloof Nature Garden** are worth visiting.

D3 5 Cape Agulhas The southernmost point of Africa. The old lighthouse is an extension of the Bredasdorp Museum.

C1 6 Ceres The town which serves a fertile deciduous fruit-producing district, boasts the largest fruit-packing house in the southern hemisphere. Worth visiting are the **Ceres Nature Reserve** and the **Transport Riders' Museum.**

A1 7 Darling Regarded as the southern limit of the famous wild flower belt. The village of **Mamre** close by, established as a mission station in 1808, has a rich heritage of Cape Dutch buildings.

B2 8 Franschhoek The area which was settled between 1688 and 1690 by French Huguenots who fled religious persecution in France is now an important wine-producing district. The **Franschhoek Wine Route** via several estates is a major attraction.

B2 9 Gordon's Bay This popular fishing harbour and holiday resort has a small sheltered beach. The scenic **Steenbras Dam** close by offers recreational facilities and accommodation.

B2 10 Grabouw Situated in the fertile Groenland Valley, Grabouw is the commercial centre of the world-famous apple-producing Elgin district. Tourist attractions include the **Apple Museum** depicting the history of the apple industry and the **Kathleen Murray Reserve,** famous for its wealth of indigenous flora.

C3 11 Hermanus A scenic and much sought after resort on the shores of Walker Bay, renowned among fishermen and water sports fans. The **Old Harbour Museum** reflects the history of the town and the **Fernkloof Nature Reserve** offers a number of signposted walks, an abundance of wild flowers and a prolific bird life. Southern right whales frequent this stretch of coastline to calve and mate. Sightings are announced by a whale crier in the town.

B3 12 Kleinmond Another popular holiday village offering good fishing. Nature lovers will enjoy the **Bot River Marsh** which supports thousands of water birds, and the **Kleinmond Coastal Nature Reserve,** notable for its indigenous vegetation.

B1 13 Malmesbury One of the largest grain-producing areas in the country. The **Kalbas Kraal Nature Reserve** is noted for its wild flowers, particularly beautiful in spring.

D1 14 Matjiesfontein A well-preserved Victorian village established as a health resort in the 19th century.

D2 15 Montagu The town is known for its fortified wines, fruit production, curative hot springs and many attractive and historic buildings.

B2 16 Paarl Serves one of the best wine-producing areas and is the site of the headquarters of the KWV, a statutory body that regulates wine production. Tours of the cellar complex are available. The town has many imposing old buildings, fascinating museums and an impressive monument to the Afrikaans language.

C2 17 Robertson An important wine-producing area known for its brandy and high quality muscadels.

B2 18 Somerset West Major town of the Hottentots Holland Basin. In the district the historic **Vergelegen Estate** with its magnificent homestead is open to the public. Wine tastings are held and wines may be purchased. There is also a tea garden, gift shop and an interpretive centre.

B2 19 Stellenbosch This historic town founded in 1679 is renowned for the gracious Cape Dutch thatched and gabled buildings and stately oaks which line the streets. It is considered one of the best preserved towns from the era of the Dutch East India Company. **Oom Samie se Winkel -** a Victorian dealer's store dating from 1904, the **Stellenbosch Village Museum, Libertas Parvas** which houses an art gallery and wine museum, and the 150-year old **Lanzerac Hotel** are some of the attractions here.

B2 20 Strand Situated on the shores of False Bay, the warm water of the Indian Ocean makes this a popular seaside resort.

D2 21 Swellendam An agricultural centre beneath the impressive Langeberg Mountains characterised by oak-lined streets and well-preserved historic buildings. The **Drostdy Museum** and **Bontebok National Park** where the rare and beautiful bontebok occurs, are well worth visiting.

B1 22 Tulbagh Much of this town was destroyed by an earthquake in 1969. The meticulously restored Cape Dutch buildings lining Church Street, constitute the largest concentration of national monuments in the country.

B1 23 Wellington Centre of the dried fruit industry at the foot of the Drakenstein Mountains. The town has a number of interesting national monuments, among them **Twistniet,** the original house on the farm Champagne on which the town was laid out, and **Clairvaux,** the house in which Dr Andrew Murray lived.

C1 24 Worcester Principal town of the Breë River Valley, surrounded by mountains that are often snow-capped in winter. The **Worcester Museum,** housed in three historic buildings, contains fascinating exhibits. Also of interest is the former home of the artist Hugo Naudé (1868-1941), the old drostdy (magistrate's residence) with its fine Regency façade and the Karoo National Botanic Garden. The **KWV Brandy Cellar,** the largest of its kind in the world, may also be visited. Conducted tours are offered.

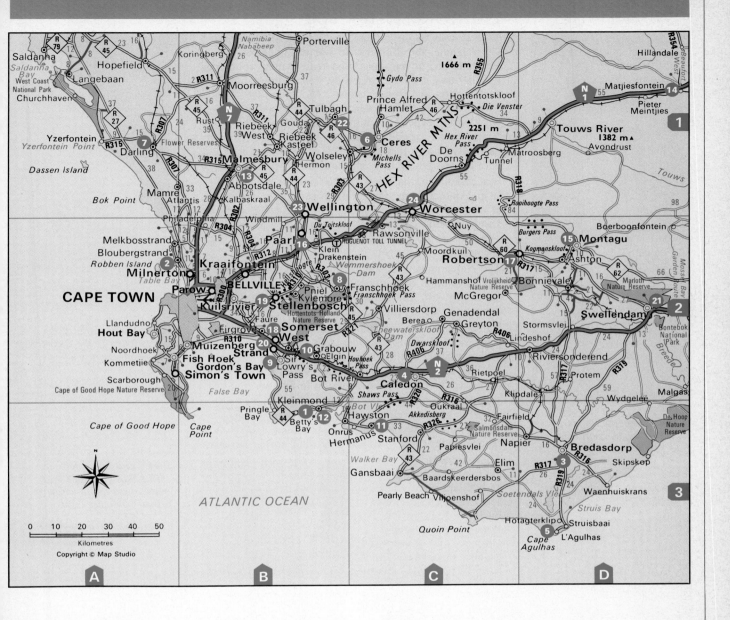

North-western Cape

Tucked away in the remote, north-western corner of the province, the Richtersveld was designed for the energetic and adventurous who really enjoy 'roughing it'. The area is characterised by steep gorges, high peaks, cliffs and frequent mists. Mod-cons are conspicuous by their absence and considerable four-wheel drive experience is required of those who undertake an expedition into the Richtersveld. It's not generally known that some 50% of the plants found here are extremely rare and endemic to the region.

Peaceful fishing harbours dot the Sandveld coastal strip. Among them, Port Nolloth overlooks the bustle of trawlers and the occasional antics of seals, while Lambert's Bay is especially recommended for bird-watchers. From a lookout platform, thousands of Cape cormorants and gannets may be observed.

The Namaqualand copper rush was the catalyst for the rapid evolution of the once undeveloped wastelands of the north-west, and mining is still carried out at Springbok, Okiep and Nababeep.

Namaqualand is Cinderella country. For much of the year, the undulating semi-desert is rather unremarkable. But after the right amount of winter rainfall, the terrain is transformed into a carpet of brilliant blooms from one horizon to another.

Travelling south from Springbok, the N7 leads through the quiet villages of Kamieskroon, Garies, Vanrhynsdorp, Vredendal and Clanwilliam, all renowned for the extravagance of their spring flowers.

Apart from the flowers, the region is notable for its brilliant night skies, fine examples of Bushman rock art, abundant deposits of semi-precious stones, and friendly hospitality.

Above: Some 50% of the plants found in the Richtersveld are extremely rare.

Below and below left: In spring, the landscape is transformed into a carpet of brilliant blooms.

Above: Lambert's Bay is renowned for its enormous congregations of Cape Gannets.

Below: Langebaan attracts sunworshippers, yachtsmen and catamaran sailors.

Above and above left: *The Cedarberg is renowned for its unusual rock formations.*

Left: *Visitors from far and wide marvel at the beauty of Namaqualand in spring.*

Right: *Delicious rock lobsters (crayfish) are found in huge numbers off the Atlantic coast.*

Above: *Peaceful fishing villages dot the narrow Sandveld coastal strip.*

Right: *Seaside resorts attract holiday-makers throughout the year.*

Places of Interest

D4 1 Calvinia Capital of the north-western Cape and one of the largest wool-producing districts in South Africa. An Art Deco style synagogue is a reminder of the strong Jewish presence in Namaqualand from the 1920s to late sixties. The synagogue now houses the **Calvinia Museum.**

C4 2 Cedarberg Mountains Characterised by gnarled cedar trees, craggy peaks and spectacular weathered rocks such as the Wolfberg Arch and Maltese Cross. The rich plant life includes spring annuals, fynbos and indigenous forest. The **Cedarberg Wilderness Area** is a popular hiking and mountaineering area. Access is via the Algeria Forest Station where permits to enter are obtained.

B5 3 Churchhaven A picturesque fishing settlement with a small beach on the banks of the Langebaan Lagoon. The **Postberg Nature Reserve** (only open in August/September) is a feast of colour in spring when the wild flowers bloom.

C5 4 Citrusdal Primarily a citrus area. There is a museum of local history in the town. Accommodation and other facilities are available at the mineral baths some 18 km from the town.

C4 5 Clanwilliam An old-world town with thatched houses and concrete streets serving a prosperous farming community; centre of the rooibos tea industry pioneered by Dr Nortier. The **Leipoldt-Nortier Memorial Library** commemorates Dr Nortier and his friend Dr Louis Leipoldt, famous South African poet, epicure and doctor. The **Ramskop Nature Reserve** and the **Clanwilliam Wild Flower Garden** adjoining the Clanwilliam Dam are beautiful in spring. The **Bidouw Valley** reached via the **Pakhuis Pass** with its unusual rock formations is also worth visiting in spring.

C4 6 Graafwater This village is the dispatch point for the agricultural products of Clanwilliam and seafood from Lambert's Bay. The area was visited by explorers from as early as 1682 when Oloff Bergh, an adventurous Swede in the employ of the Dutch East India Company, came in search of the mythical goldfields of Monomotapa.

B2 7 Kamieskroon The village is renowned for the variety and wealth of its wild flowers in spring. A photographic workshop/safari is conducted annually in spring from the local hotel.

B4 8 Lambert's Bay A picturesque fishing village and important fish-processing centre on the Crayfish Route. **Bird Island,** joined to the mainland by a pier, is inhabited by over 150 bird species. The **Sandveld Museum** depicts the history of the area.

B5 9 Langebaan A fishing village at the head of a large shallow lagoon of the same name and a popular venue for yachting, boardsailing and catamaranning. The lagoon and surrounding area comprise the **West Coast National Park** which is internationally recognised as one of the great wetlands of the world. The park is especially noted for its prolific bird life and in summer is populated by some 55,000 birds. These include cormorants, gulls, sandpipers, plovers, gannets and flamingoes.

C5 10 Moorreesburg Situated in the heart of the grain belt and home of the **Wheat Industry Museum's** interesting exhibits.

C4 11 Nieuwoudtville Due to its location on a plateau which receives a higher rainfall than the surrounding area, the display of spring wild flowers here is exquisite. Elegant sandstone buildings line the village streets. The **Nieuwoudtville Wild Flower Reserve, Nieuwoudtville Falls** and **Vanrhyns Pass** in the district are all worth viewing. Of particular interest is the forest of quiver trees (*Aloe dichotoma*) on the road from Nieuwoudtville to Loeriesfontein.

B5 12 Paternoster A peaceful fishing village with quaint whitewashed cottages over 100 years old. Rock lobsters are caught, processed and exported from here.

A2 13 Port Nolloth Desert port and holiday resort serving the northern Cape. Centre for alluvial diamond industry and thriving fishing industry. Good line fishing and crayfishing.

A1 14 Richtersveld The area is noted for its dramatic mountain desert scenery with ornate wind-sculpted rock formations. Motorists may travel between Port Nolloth and Alexander Bay but require a permit to leave the road. (Obtainable from the Richtersveld Management Committee in Lekkersing or Khubus.)

B5 15 Saldanha An industrial iron-ore export harbour, fish-processing centre and water sports venue.

B2 16 Springbok Capital of Namaqualand. The **Goegap Nature Reserve** is noted for its indigenous flora, particularly succulents, and also has a succulent nursery. The reserve is at its best in spring.

B4 17 Strandfontein A popular resort on this section of the coast offering good swimming, surfing and fishing. Diamonds are recovered from the sea at De Punt by unique methods.

D4 18 Sutherland Coldest town in the country with a mean minimum temperature of -6.1° and heavy snowfalls in winter. It is the principal astronomical centre in Africa. The **South African Astronomical Observatory** is situated about 14 km outside the town.

C4 19 Vanrhynsdorp The district is renowned for its succulents and spring-flowering daisies. A succulent nursery is one of the town's main attractions.

B5 20 Velddrif-Laaiplek A fishing centre and popular water sports venue on the Berg River. Pelicans and flamingoes are often seen.

B5 21 Vredenburg The commercial centre of a sheep and wheat-farming area. The **Cape Columbine Nature Reserve** is the site of the only manually operated lighthouse in the country.

C4 22 Vredendal Centre of the Olifants River Irrigation Scheme, the town is surrounded by vineyards and orchards. In a good year Vredendal has wonderful displays of wild flowers.

C4 23 Wuppertal A small village which grew around the **Rhenish Mission Station** (established in 1830). It has quaint whitewashed cottages and a fine gabled church. Comfortable walking shoes known as 'velskoene' are manufactured locally.

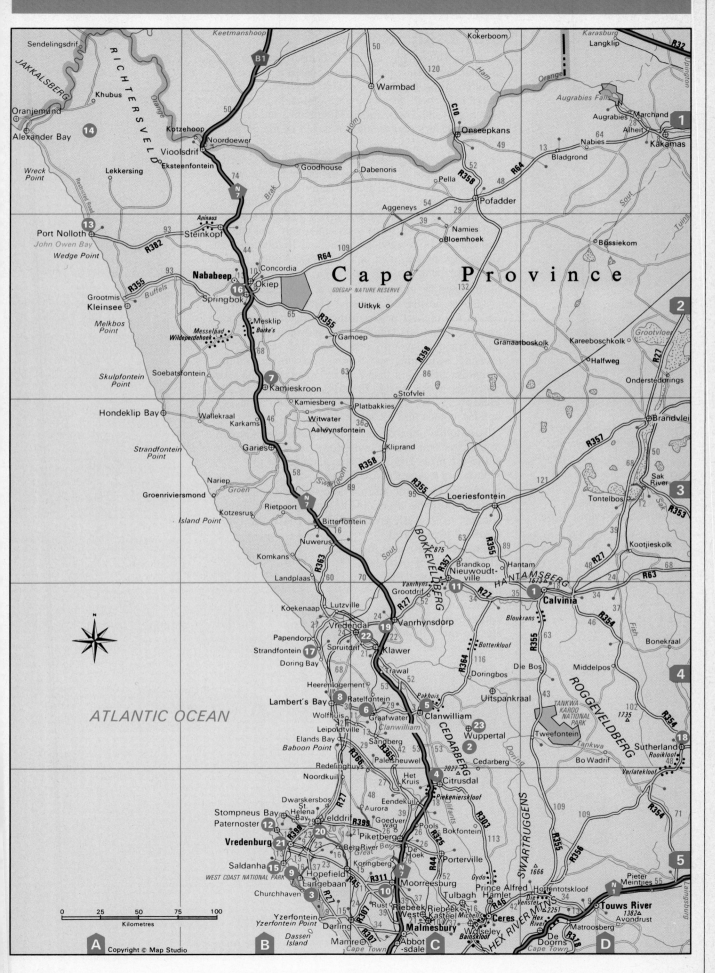

Garden Route and Little Karoo

Between Mossel Bay and the Storms River, the Garden Route runs parallel to a coastline which features lakes, mountains, golden beaches, cliffs and dense indigenous forests. From sources high in the Outeniqua and Tsitsikamma Mountains, amber-coloured rivers plunge into an ocean of mercurial moods.

On this enchanting stretch of coast, holiday resorts from the simple to the luxurious cater for fitness fanatics as well as the unashamedly indolent. Secluded coves such as Herolds Bay and Victoria Bay, and the long beaches of Wilderness, Sedgefield and Buffels Bay attract those who enjoy sun, sea and a laid back holiday agenda. Scheduled flights link George (principal town of the Garden Route) with all the major centres in the country.

Surrounded by indigenous forests, the delightful town of George nestles on a coastal plateau at the foot of one of the highest peaks in the Outeniqua mountain range. Knysna has fabulous sea and mountain views and a tranquil lagoon - one of the finest sailing, cruising, swimming and fishing spots in the country. Connoisseurs claim that Knysna oysters are the most succulent in the world. In addition to golden beaches, Plettenberg Bay features trendy boutiques, affluent holiday homes and jet set hotels.

Hikers follow meandering trails through the Garden Route; the rain forests invite long, leisurely drives, while the lakes and rivers lend themselves to swimming, boating and fishing.

Capital of the Little Karoo, Oudtshoorn is easily reached over the streamlined Outeniqua Pass. In contrast to the lush greenery of the coast, the Little Karoo is a semi-arid valley which provides the ideal habitat for ostriches. 'Feather Palaces', built at the turn of the century, are reminders of an opulent era when feathers fetched more than their weight in gold.

Top: Tsitsikamma Forest – an area of streams and lush greenery.

Above: The Cape clawless otter is sometimes seen in the region.

Below: Up-market hotel, Beacon Island, Plettenberg Bay.

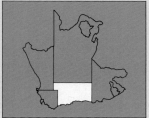

Left: *Shopping in Knysna is a leisurely, laid-back occupation.*

Above: *Knysna Lagoon — the perfect place for water sports.*

Above right: *Rich farmlands near Uniondale in the Long Kloof.*

Right: *Hikers follow meandering trails through the Garden Route.*

Below: *Holiday chalets, Tsitsikamma National Park.*

Top: *Oudtshoorn is famous for its flourishing ostrich farms.*

Above: *The Cango Caves rank among the wonders of the world.*

Below left: *The Storms River Mouth in a gentle mood.*

Below: *Exquisite shells can be found along the coastline.*

Places of Interest

B1 1 Beaufort West
Capital of the vast semi-arid region known as the Karoo. Outstanding buildings are the Gothic-style Dutch Reformed church and the museum complex consisting of the old town hall, the adjoining old mission church and the parsonage. The **Karoo National Park** is noted for its unique Karoo flora and is well-stocked with game. Accommodation and a restaurant are available. The **Springbok Hiking Trail** traverses the park; overnight huts are provided.

C4 2 Buffels Bay
This holiday resort is noted for its beautiful sandy beach which stretches to **Brenton-on-Sea.**

A3 3 Calitzdorp
The town overlooks the lush wine and fruit-producing Gamka River Valley. Wine tastings are offered at Die Krans and Boplaas Estates. There is a mineral spa close by.

B3 4 Cango Caves
Regarded as one of South Africa's foremost natural wonders, the fascinating calcite caves comprise an underground wonderland of stalactites and stalagmites. Tours are conducted into the caves. A restaurant, curio shop and crèche are available at the entrance.

B4 5 George Scenically situated on a coastal plateau at the foot of the Outeniqua Mountains. The **George Museum,** housed in the old drostdy, includes a splendid collection of Victorian bric-a-brac. Steam enthusiasts should not miss a ride on the **Outeniqua Choo-Tjoe,** one of the few remaining steam trains in the country. It runs between George and Knysna. Two scenic passes, the Outeniqua and Montagu, link George to the interior.

E4 6 Jeffrey's Bay
A popular holiday resort, especially among surfers. The almost rock-free coastline is noted for its shells. The local library also houses a fine collection of sea shells.

D3 7 Joubertina
The main centre of the Langkloof where fruit, mainly for export, is produced.

D4 8 Kareedouw
A timber and farming centre. The mountain slopes to the south of the town are rich in fynbos; explore them along a scenic circular drive that starts from Keet Street.

C4 9 Knysna This well-known holiday resort on the Garden Route was established by George Rex, reputedly the son of George III. The town lies on the **Knysna Lagoon,** the mouth of which is guarded by two promontories known as **The Heads.** The lagoon is an excellent venue for water sports and pleasure and cabin cruises are available. Other attractions include the **Featherbed Nature Reserve** and the **Millwood House Museum.** Vast tracts of indigenous forests occur around Knysna.

B3 10 Meiringspoort
A spectacular 20-km gorge through the Swartberg Range. A feature of these mountains is the dramatic folding of the sandstone strata which is clearly visible in the towering cliffs flanking the road.

B4 11 Mossel Bay Site of the first landfall made by the Portuguese explorer Bartholomeu Dias in 1488 and today a popular holiday resort with fine beaches and much else to offer the tourist. The **Bartholomeu Dias Museum Complex** comprises historical, maritime and shell museums. Launch trips are offered to nearby **Seal Island** with its noisy population of some 2,000 seals as well as gannets and cormorants.

C4 12 Nature's Valley
Mainly a village of private holiday homes in beautiful surroundings with a long stretch of beach.

B3 13 Oudtshoorn
Known as the 'Feather Capital' of the world because of the large ostrich industry in the area. Attractions include two ostrich show farms **Highgate** and **Safari** and **Arbeidsgenot,** the home of poet and writer C J Langenhoven which is preserved as a museum. The **C P Nel Museum** in town is also worth visiting. At the **Cango Crocodile Ranch and Cheetahland,** besides crocodiles cheetahs and a snake park, lions, pumas and jaguars can be viewed.

E4 14 Oyster Bay
A beautiful wide beach is the main attraction at this popular holiday resort. Sea otters inhabit the nature reserve between Oyster Bay and Cape St Francis.

D4 15 Paul Sauer Bridge
Towering 139 m above the Storms River, the impressive bridge is a popular stop along the Garden Route.

C4 16 Plettenberg Bay
An up-market resort with three magnificent beaches. The **Robberg Nature Reserve** is noted for its varied coastal vegetation, rich inter-tidal life and many bird species.

A4 17 Riversdale
Riversdale boasts many old buildings such as **Versveld House** which houses the **Julius Gordon Africana Museum** with its beautiful antique furniture and paintings. Also of interest is the **Jurisch Park Wild Flower Garden.**

E4 18 St Francis Bay
A vast bay encompassing the popular seaside resorts of **Cape St Francis, Paradise Beach** and **Aston Bay,** all with wide unspoilt beaches. The **Seekoei River Nature Reserve** at Aston Bay accommodates many species of waterfowl, and the **Cape St Francis Marine Nature**

Reserve, the South African sea otter.

A3 19 Swartberg Pass
An impressive mountain pass linking the Little Karoo to the Great Karoo. A series of hair-raising bends yields spectacular views. **Prince Albert** at the foot of the pass is known for its lovely old buildings of varied architectural styles.

D4 20 Tsitsikamma Forest Dense, indigenous forest renowned for a large number of giant yellowwood and stinkwood trees, forest ferns, clear streams, magnificent birds and fascinating walks.

D4 21 Tsitsikamma National Park This park comprises a glorious 100-km stretch of wild and rocky coastline characterised by massive cliffs, narrow isolated beaches and shady indigenous forest along the river valleys. The five-day **Otter Trail** starts at Storms River and ends at the Groot River Mouth near Nature's Valley. An underwater trail for swimmers, skindivers and scuba enthusiasts is a major attraction. There are self-catering chalets and camping facilities at the mouth of the Storms River.

B4 22 Wilderness National Park The attractive lake area stretching eastwards from the picturesque village of Wilderness comprises the **Touw River Estuary,** the **Serpentine Channel, Eilandvlei, Langvlei,** **Rondevlei** and **Swartvlei.** The area is a paradise for bird-watchers and water sports enthusiasts.

Eastern Cape

Whether you're in the mood for an informal seaside escape from office routine or something more sophisticated, you'll find what you're looking for on the eastern Cape coast.

Between Kei Mouth and Jeffrey's Bay (one of the world's best surfing spots), holiday resorts follow a weather-beaten coastline much frequented by fishermen. Many comprise only a cluster of houses, shops, bowling greens, tennis courts and a small hotel or two. Peace you'll have in abundance, space and an exuberant sparkling ocean.

Port Alfred, on the Kowie River, offers forest trails and rolling surf. Anglers gravitate to the shoreline, river and rocks; sunworshippers gather on sweeping sandy beaches on both sides of the river.

From Port Alfred, it's an easy drive to Grahamstown, brimful with charm and a gracious historical ambience. Apart from Church Square's outstanding examples of Victorian architecture, there is much to see and admire in Grahamstown, and most of your exploration can be done on foot. Westward, the Karoo town of Graaff-Reinet, with its old gabled, green-shuttered houses and perfectly restored Cape Dutch hotel, provides an ideal stopover spot for excursions into the surrounding countryside. Farm holidays are a special attraction in the eastern Cape.

Let your spirit of adventure lead you further afield into the wonderland known as Hogsback - an enchantment of forests, mountain streams and waterfalls.

When pleasures of a more worldly kind appeal, you'll find plenty to amuse you in Port Elizabeth and East London. Both are year-round family resorts, large enough to offer all of the amenities of a city, yet small enough to be genuinely welcoming and friendly. They also provide quick and convenient access to unspoilt areas of natural beauty.

Top: *The landscape is dotted about with flame-coloured aloes.*

Above: *Inhabitants of the Mountain Zebra National Park.*

Below: *Port Alfred — a charming eastern Cape holiday resort.*

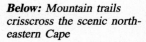

Above: *Riding the waves at Jeffrey's Bay.*

Below: *Mountain trails crisscross the scenic north-eastern Cape*

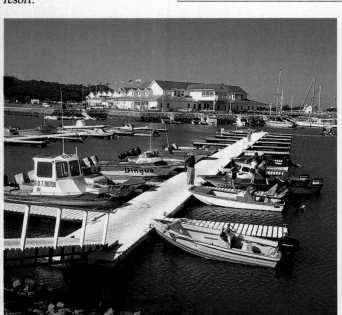

Left: The Addo Elephant National Park, near Port Elizabeth.

Below left: The charming city of Grahamstown has a gracious, historical ambience.

Right: Stretch's Court, Graaff-Reinet, offers fine accommodation.

Below: Bathurst lies at the hub of a prosperous agricultural area in Settler Country.

Left: The Wild Coast Sun occupies a prime site on Transkei's coast.

Below left: Blue chip options at the Wild Coast Casino.

Below: Xhosa women adorn themselves with elaborate beadwork.

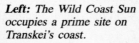

Places of Interest

B4 1 Addo Elephant National Park The densely vegetated natural habitat of the park supports close on 180 elephants. In addition black rhino, buffalo, rhino, eland, red hartebeest, kudu and more than 170 bird species occur in the park. Night drives are offered on request. Accommodation and a restaurant are available.

C3 2 Adelaide A wool, mohair, grain and citrus-producing centre. **Our Heritage Museum** contains lovely furniture and fine collections of glass, porcelain and silver.

C1 3 Aliwal North Popular hot spring with several pools and a biokinetic centre. The two museums (in the Buffelsvlei farmhouse near the spa and the old library building in town), Bushman paintings in the district and the **Buffelspruit Game Reserve** are of interest to tourists.

D1 4 Barkly East Situated in the Witteberg Range and known as the Switzerland of South Africa, the town is a favourite skiing venue in winter. In summer, trout angling is equally popular. A unique railway line links the town to Lady Grey: to descend the steep gradient, the train negotiates eight reverses.

C4 5 Bathurst The village lies in a cattle-farming and pineapple-growing district. The **Agricultural Museum** depicts the history of agriculture in the area, and **Bradshaw's Mill** symbolises the modest start of South Africa's wool industry. The **Horseshoe Bend Nature Reserve** conserves small antelope and many birds. **Summerhill Farm** close by is a model pineapple farm with many attractions for young and old.

C1 6 Burgersdorp A wool and livestock-farming centre with historical associations and several national monuments. The **J L de Bruin Dam** offers water sports and camping. **Die Berg Nature Reserve** is home to various species of buck and other small mammals.

B2 7 Cradock Established in 1813 as a military outpost, Cradock is now a town of considerable charm. Visit the splendid **Dutch Reformed Church,** a replica of St Martins-in-the-Field in London, the **Great Fish River Museum** and **Olive Schreiner House** where memorabilia of this famous writer can be seen. A mineral spa close by offers accommodation and other amenities.

D2 8 Elliot Stunning views of the Drakensberg and winter snowfalls await visitors to Elliot. Places to visit include **Thompson Dam** and the gallery of Bushman paintings on the farm **Denorbin.**

C3 9 Fort Beaufort A local history museum, military museum and the **Martello Tower** attest to the military past of the town.

A3 10 Graaff-Reinet The oldest town in the eastern Cape is recommended for the number and grace of its restored buildings. These include the **Drostdy Hotel,** museum complex, **Hester Rupert Art Museum, Jan Rupert Centre, Stretch's Court** and many beautiful old homes. In all there are 220 proclaimed national monuments.

C3 11 Grahamstown Situated in the heart of Settler Country and steeped in history, this gracious old cathedral city has much to offer. A host of museums, quaint settler cottages, fine Georgian buildings and no less than 40 churches will intrigue visitors.

C3 12 Hogsback Situated high in the Amatola Mountains, the charm of this village lies in the scenic beauty of the area. Well-marked paths lead through cool indigenous forests which are transformed into a fairyland after winter snowfalls.

A3 13 Karoo Nature Reserve The reserve embraces the **Valley of Desolation** with its sculpted dolerite pinnacles and domes. The area stocked with game is only open during weekends and holiday periods. Various trails and walks lead through the reserve.

D3 14 King William's Town Visitors will find the rich historical legacy of the town and interesting museums such as the **Kaffrarian Museum** and the **Missionary Museum** fascinating.

D2 15 Maclear Trout fishing and hiking are popular pursuits. Trails range from day walks to five-day hikes. Skiing in winter and water-skiing on the **Maclear Dam** in summer also appeal.

B3 16 Mountain Zebra National Park Established to ensure the survival of the Cape mountain zebra, the park is also home to a variety of other game. Accommodation is available.

C4 17 Port Alfred A popular holiday resort offering good swimming, surfing and angling. The 24-km **Kowie Canoe Trail** is a novel way of exploring the **Kowie Nature Reserve.**

C2 18 Queenstown A town famed for its beautiful roses. Tourist attractions include the **Queenstown and Frontier Museum,** two art galleries, sunken gardens and the annual rose show. The **Bongola Dam** offers water sports while the **J de Lange Game Reserve** conserves a variety of antelope and indigenous plant life.

D1 19 Rhodes A winter holiday retreat with seasonal snowfalls and skiing. Trout fishing, riding, hiking and partridge shooting in season are popular pastimes.

B3 20 Somerset East In this sheep and angora goat-farming area there are delightful mountain drives and walks to nearby forests. The **Walter Battiss Art Gallery** in town displays works by the renowned South African artist.

D3 21 Stutterheim Mountains, rivers and woodlands provide a scenic setting for a town steeped in history. Walks and trails are available in the nearby **Kologha** and **Kubusi Forests.**

B4 22 Uitenhage Fascinating museums housed in **Cuyler Manor,** the **Old Drostdy** and the **Old Railway Station** prove that Uitenhage is not just an industrial offshoot of Port Elizabeth. **Canon Hill Garden** is noted for its succulents and cactuses.

B4 23 Van Staden's Pass and Wildflower Reserve The scenic pass on the Old Cape Way and lovely walks in the wildflower reserve make it worth deviating from the N2 highway.

B4 24 Zuurberg National Park Dense indigenous forests and Cape fynbos support a natural population of grey rhebok, mountain reedbuck, bushbuck, duiker and many birds.

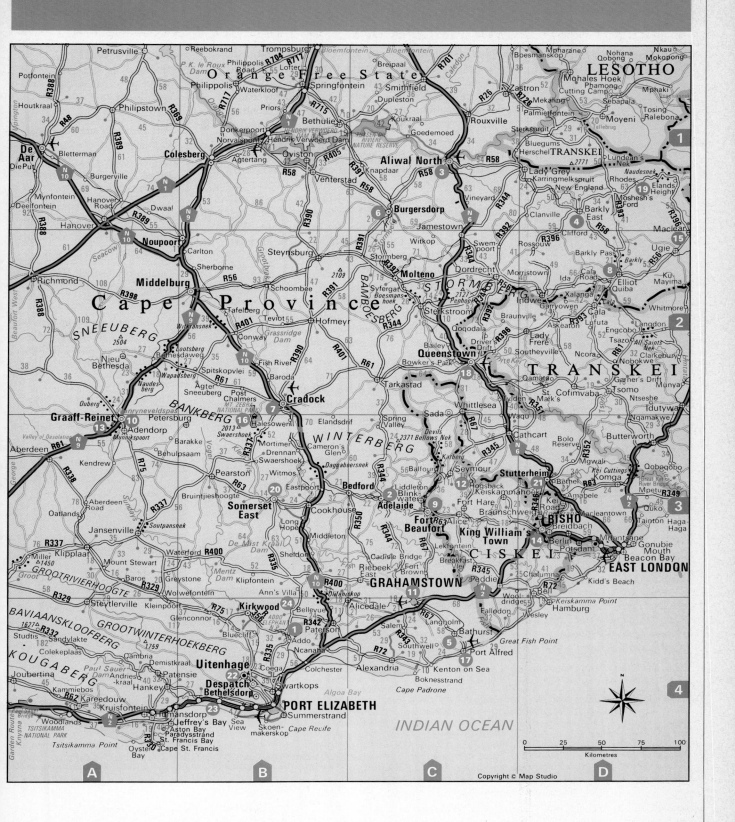

Port Elizabeth

Only a few minutes away from the city centre, the beaches on the long graceful sweep of Algoa Bay provide unlimited opportunities throughout the year for swimming, rock and surf angling, deep sea fishing, boating, surfing and diving. The yachting fraternity tends to gravitate to Hobie Beach and the placid waters of the Swartkops River.

Land-based sportsmen have access to tennis and squash courts, bowling greens and championship golf courses. Spectator sports include rugby, horse racing, motocross and motor racing. Museums, historical buildings, parks, botanical gardens and nature reserves offer unlimited opportunities for exploration. Within the boundaries of the city itself, strollers through Settlers Park Nature Reserve will marvel at its wildness and prolific bird life.

Don't miss the engaging antics of dolphins and seals at the Oceanarium. At the same venue, the Snake Park houses exotic and indigenous reptiles, while the Tropical House is inhabited by colourful birds. Entertainment after dark encompasses theatre, opera, cabaret and disco.

In the vicinity, the fruit-producing Long Kloof valley is well worth a leisurely drive. When the orchards are in blossom, the valley is particularly beautiful and during the picking season, the fragrance of fruit fills the air.

Wildlife enthusiasts have a treat in store. In addition to the Addo Elephant and Mountain Zebra National Parks, two up-market private reserves are within easy driving distance of Port Elizabeth.

Suggested Tours

The following scheduled tours depart on a regular basis from Port Elizabeth:

Port Elizabeth City

Port Elizabeth and Uitenhage Highlights

Garden Route (Tsitsikamma, Jeffrey's Bay, Storms River, Nature's Valley)

Addo Elephant National Park/ Mountain Zebra National Park

Grahamstown - Settler Country

The Karoo

Oudtshoorn/Ostrich Farm/ Cango Caves/Crocodile Farm

Transkei

Visitors with transport have the advantage of flexibility and a great many additional options, including the following:

Scenic Drives

There are many scenic drives in the vicinity, particularly along the coast and through the rolling countryside to the west.

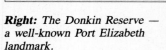

Top: *Don't miss the engaging antics of dolphins at the Port Elizabeth Oceanarium.*

Above: *Port Elizabeth's horse memorial.*

Below: *Historic Market Square.*

Right: *The Donkin Reserve — a well-known Port Elizabeth landmark.*

Below right: *Steam train buffs ride the Apple Express through the Long Kloof valley.*

The drive north-west of the city through the Elands River Valley and the Van Staden's River Gorge is particularly beautiful.

Mpekweni Sun Marine Reserve/Fish River Sun (Ciskei: 150 km east of Port Elizabeth) see page 105.

Coastal Resorts
West of Port Elizabeth, St Francis Bay, with its legendary waves and abundant fishing waters, is one of the prime recreational areas of the eastern Cape. Jeffrey's Bay and St Francis Bay attract holiday-makers throughout the year, and surfers from all over the world gravitate to the area. Westward, the Tsitsikamma Forest, Storms River and Nature's Valley are well worth a visit.

Addo Elephant National Park (72 kilometres north of Port Elizabeth)
Covers 12,000 ha of bush and is home to about 145 elephants,

as well as buffalo, rhino, buck and ostrich. Accommodation is available.

Mountain Zebra National Park (27 kilometres west of Cradock)
In addition to mountain zebra, there are large herds of eland, springbok, blesbok, black wildebeest, kudu, steenbok and red hartebeest. Carnivores include caracal, African wild cat, black-backed jackal and Cape fox. Two hundred bird species have been recorded, including a breeding population of black eagle.

Settler Country
The country between the Karoo and the Great Kei River is studded with small towns of historic and architectural interest; these include Fort Brown, Fort Beaufort, Bathurst, King William's Town and Grahamstown.

Picturesque Grahamstown (128 km north-east of Port Elizabeth) nestles among

pleasant hills in the heart of Settler Country. The town has the serenity and elegance of a typical English cathedral town. Historical buildings include tiny cottages built by the early British settlers, and splendid examples of Victorian architecture. Grahamstown provides easy access to historic towns and forts in the surrounding area.

Graaff-Reinet (296 km north of Port Elizabeth) is as close to perfection as any small town could hope to be. The streets, lined with shady trees and colourful flowers, are the setting for meticulously

restored historic buildings. They include gems of Cape Dutch, Victorian and Karoo architecture (a simplified Cape Dutch style).

For further information on tours and details of tour operators, restaurants, shopping centres, specialist shops and accommodation, contact your nearest SATOUR office (see back cover) or the Port Elizabeth Publicity Association (see page 121).

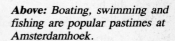

Above: Boating, swimming and fishing are popular pastimes at Amsterdamhoek.

Above: Port Elizabeth's lighthouse, built in 1861, is no longer in use.

Right: Algoa Bay provides unlimited opportunities for every type of water sport.

Left: The yachting fraternity gravitates to Hobie Beach and the Swartkops River.

East London

Situated on one of the most attractive stretches of coastline on the eastern seaboard, East London's broad beaches extend for miles - unpolluted, uncrowded, unspoilt. Swimming, sailing, water-skiing, boardsailing and boating are enjoyed all year round, while the river mouths, lagoons and gullies provide a paradise for fishermen.

East Londoners are extremely conservation-conscious, and several well-preserved examples of 19th century architecture enhance the charm of the city.

An excellent collection of South African and imported works of art is on permanent exhibition at the Ann Bryant Art Gallery, while paintings and graphics by artists of international repute are regularly displayed.

Occupying pride of place at East London's museum, the famous prehistoric coelacanth caught in the Chalumna River in 1938, was previously thought to have been extinct for 50 million years.

Quiet seaside resorts such as Haga Haga and Morgan's Bay are reached by car within an hour. On the western side of the Buffalo River, Igoda, Gulu and Kidd's Beach can hardly be matched for tranquil loveliness. Hogsback, in the Amatola Mountains, is a favourite among nature lovers and climbers.

And when the sun goes down on the city, there are theatres, cinemas, and a selection of restaurants to pamper the discerning palate. But if it's the one-armed bandits you crave, Bisho's casino is less than an hour's drive away.

Suggested Tours

The following scheduled tours depart on a regular basis from East London:

City Highlights

Scenic Excursion (East)

Scenic Excursion (West)

Pineapple Trail/Reptile World/Research Station

Mpongo Park/Calgary Trail/Transport Museum

Visitors with transport have the advantage of flexibility and a great many additional options, including the following:

Amatola Crafts Amble

An arts and crafts route which spans Hogsback, Happy Valley, Cathcart and Stutterheim. Encompasses the products of weaving, spinning, sculpting and pottery, as well as art, antiques and furniture. Bird-watching, fishing and hiking opportunities and comfortable country hotels invite you to explore at leisure.

Above: *East London's City Hall, flanked by an Anglo-Boer War memorial.*
Below: *The city is situated on a most attractive stretch of the eastern seaboard.*
Below right: *Between Transkei and Ciskei, the beaches are uncrowded and pristine clean.*

Above: *Snakes and crocs are the star attractions at Reptile World.*

Right: *A memorial to some 2,000 Germans who arrived in the area between 1858 and 1859.*

Amatola Sun (Ciskei: just outside Bisho)

A casino resort, the Amatola Sun provides a wide range of sports facilities and excursions to the Amatola Mountains.

Eagle's Ridge Forest Resort (Reached by a turn-off from the R352 between Stutterheim and Keiskammahoek.)

The resort has splendid views across a valley to the slopes of the Kologha State Forests. A two-day trail takes hikers past cliffs where eagles nest. Nights are spent in a large hut.

Hogsback (Less than an hour and a half by road from East London.)

A charming resort at the western end of the thickly forested Amatola mountains, dominated by three mountain peaks resembling the bristle-backed wild hogs of the forest. Hogsback's charm lies in its mountain air, in country lanes, giant yellowwoods, ferns, wild

flowers and edible berries; in waterfalls, mountain streams and birdsong. The area is also noteworthy because of its excellent trout fishing conditions.

Coastal Resorts

Between Transkei and Ciskei, the 200-km coastline is dotted with unspoilt holiday resorts acclaimed by fishermen. There are fish to be caught throughout the year and catch records abound in the area. Most resorts cater for sports enthusiasts. All have pristine clean beaches, rampant subtropical vegetation, a wealth of indigenous bird life and wonderful views. Those who enjoy solitude will find it at Kei Mouth, Morgan's Bay, Haga Haga or Cintsa on the east coast.

Mpekweni Sun Marine Resort/Fish River Sun (Ciskei: some 124 km west of East London)

Two resort complexes within eight kilometres of each other on the unspoilt Ciskei coast offer luxury accommodation and other facilities. Daytime entertainment is Mpekweni's speciality, from water-skiing, windsurfing, canoeing and riverboat cruises, to deep sea fishing, tennis, bowls, squash and snooker, bird-watching and nature trails. At the Fish River Sun, you can experience the thrill of the casino, play golf on the championship 18-hole golf course designed by Gary Player, or go horse riding along the unspoilt beach.

One-hour or half-day beachcomber trips in four-wheel drive vehicles enable you

to explore the coastline as far as Hamburg.

Mpongo Park Game Reserve (29 km north-west of East London)

Sanctuary for lion, rhino, giraffe, zebra, blue wildebeest, kudu and nyala. You can follow the game trails by car, on foot or on horseback. (The lions are kept in an enclosure.) Some people opt for the obvious advantages of a four-wheel drive vehicle and the services of an experienced guide.

For further information on tours and details of tour operators, restaurants, shopping centres, specialist shops and accommodation, contact your nearest SATOUR office (see back cover) or the Greater East London Publicity Association (see page 121).

Top: Pleasure craft at anchor in Buffalo Harbour.

Above: The old gaol has been turned into a shopping complex.

Below: Calgary Farm features a blacksmith and wheelwright shop.

Places of Interest

B4 1 Air Terminal A bus service operates between the terminal and Ben Schoeman Airport.

A1 2 Amalinda Fisheries Station and Nature Reserve Situated just out of town off the N2 to King William's Town. The old Amalinda reservoir is stocked with a variety of fish. Sailing, canoeing and fishing are permitted. No motor boats are allowed. The nature reserve is home to a large herd of southern reedbuck and a prolific bird life, especially waterfowl.

A2 3 Ann Bryant Art Gallery Once the home of the art-collecting Bryant family, this splendid building now houses excellent collections of contemporary and old South African art, as well as English paintings.

D4 4 Aquarium Some 400 species of marine life, including great white sharks and sea horses are on display at the aquarium. Top billing probably goes to the penguins and seals. The seals perform twice daily at 11:30 and 15:30. The fish are fed daily at 10:30 and 15:00.

A5 5 Ben Schoeman Airport

A5 6 Bridle Drift Dam and Nature Reserve. Situated some 25 km from East London on the Mount Coke Road. Power boating, yachting, wind-surfing and canoeing are allowed. A boat ride to the high cliffs on the far side of the dam forms part of the Fish Eagle Trail. Canoes are available for hire and there is an overnight hut.

A5 7 Buffalo Bridge Completed in 1935, this bridge is the only two-tier road and rail bridge in the country.

D1 8 Calgary Farm About 35 km from the city on the road to Macleantown, the farm features a fine collection of antique carts and wagons as well as a blacksmith and wheelwright shop.

B4 9 City Hall A stately building in the Victorian Renaissance style.

B5 10 Deep Sea Fishing and Pleasure Cruises Cruises depart from the bay. Details are available from the Publicity Association.

D3 11 Eastern Beach Warmed by the Mozambique current, the beach offers safe bathing and surfing.

A1 12 East London Museum The museum accommodates many interesting exhibits, but the most noteworthy is the famous coelacanth, a pre-historic four-legged fish once thought to have been extinct.

C5 13 East London Yacht Club The club hosts many regattas held off the coast and is the finish of the annual Vasco da Gama Yacht Race between Durban and East London.

B4 14 Gately House Built in simple colonial style, the house was one of the first on the east bank of the Buffalo River. Today it is a house museum containing the furnishings of the Gately family.

A1 15 Guild Theatre Ballet, opera, music and drama productions are staged here regularly.

B5 16 Harbour Tours of the harbour, the only river port in the country, are arranged by the Greater East London Publicity Association. An interesting aspect of the harbour is the 'dolos' - a breakwater which consists of pieces of cast concrete resembling a stubby anchor developed by harbour engineer Eric Merrifield and now used worldwide. Piled together they break up the action of the waves.

D3 17 Marina Glen This popular picnic area has a tea garden and children's playground with a miniature railway.

D1 18 Mpongo Game Park Situated in the Mpongo Valley some 29 km north-west of East London, the park is home to a variety of game and offers good bird-watching. Amenities include a curio shop, museum and restaurant.

D1 19 Nahoon Beach On the southern bank of the Nahoon River, the beach draws swimmers and anglers. The reef off Nahoon Point creates ideal conditions for surfing.. An area of mud flats and mangroves upstream from the mouth of the Nahoon River is an important breeding ground for waterbirds.

C4 20 Old Lock Street Gaol The old gaol complex has been converted into an up-market shopping centre with interesting speciality shops. Some cells, complete with bars, can still be seen.

C5 21 Orient Beach This beach is closest to the city centre. In addition to its bathing beach, it has a waterslide, children's playground, paddling pool and a good view of ships entering and leaving the harbour. There is also a putt-putt course.

A4 22 Queens Park Botanical Garden and Zoo The attractive garden contains an abundance of indigenous plants and the zoo a variety of mammals and reptiles. Pony-rides are very popular.

B4 23 Railway Station The railway station dating from 1877 is one of the oldest buildings in the city. The steam engine on view was built in England.

A5 24 Reptile World A visit to this farm some 20 km from East London, makes for an interesting outing. The farm overlooks the Bridle Drift Dam and has a tea garden. Snake handling demonstrations take place daily at 11:30, 13:30 and 15:30. The crocodiles are fed at 15:00 on Wednesdays and Sundays in summer.

D1 25 Soffiantini Castle This prominent landmark overlooking the Nahoon Valley resembles an Italian fortress.

D4 26 Wreck Diving Diving expeditions to explore the many shipwrecks off the East London coast are available. Enquire at Pollock's Sport Shop. An appropriate certificate of competency is required.

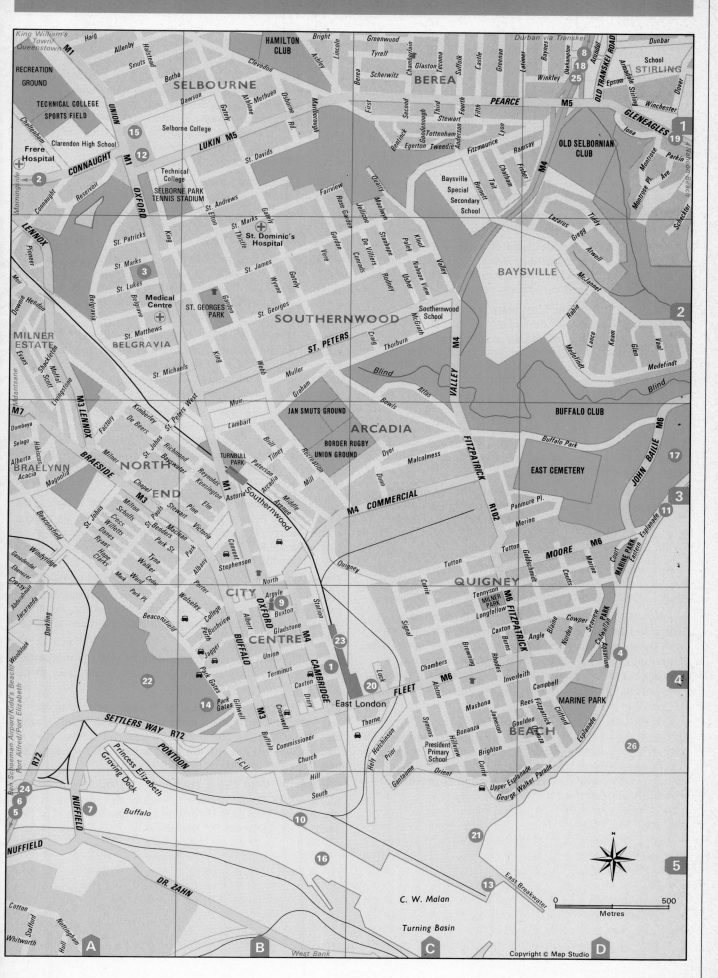

Places of Interest

Republic of Ciskei

A3 1 Amatola Hiking Trail The 104-km long trail traverses indigenous and exotic forests on the slopes of the Amatola Mountains and provides an opportunity to climb the main peaks. The forests harbour a great many bird species including the colourful Cape parrot and Knysna lourie, as well as buck, the giant golden mole and the endangered giant earthworm. Overnight accommodation and facilities are provided.

B3 2 Bisho The capital of Ciskei boasts an international hotel and casino and provides uninterrupted views of the Amatola Mountains.

A3 3 Dimbaza A wide range of goods are manufactured in this industrial township. Of special interest to tourists are the factories where handwoven karakul and other woollen rugs and carpets are produced.

A3 4 Fort Hare The University overlooking the town of Alice was named after Fort Hare which was built in 1847 at the end of the War of the Axe, one of the many frontier wars which raged in the eastern Cape. The remains of the fort may be seen in the university grounds. The **F S Malan Museum** on campus has displays of traditional costumes, charms, medicine and contemporary black art.

A4 5 Great Fish River Mouth Rock sculptures consisting of wind and wave-eroded caves and tunnels, are well worth exploring. The wetlands on the west bank attract many waterbirds. A hotel and casino complex offer a wide range of facilities.

A3 6 Katberg The forests and hills of the area make Katberg a favourite holiday area for climbers and hikers. The Katberg Pass over the mountains offers excellent views of the area.

A4 7 Mpekweni Estuary Wide beaches and endless opportunities for water sports on the lagoon draw visitors to this beautiful stretch of coastline. A marine resort offers luxury accommodation and a wide range of facilities.

A4, B4 8 Shipwreck Trail This trail leads for a distance of 64 km along the wild, unspoilt Ciskei coast from the Great Fish River Mouth to the Ncera River. The area is noted for its sandy shores, rich coastal bush, beautiful estuaries, prolific bird life and excellent fishing. There are no overnight huts along the trail; hikers camp on the beach.

A3 9 Tsolwana Game Reserve The reserve accommodates a variety of game including the exotic fallow deer. Hunting, including bow-hunting, may be enjoyed. Wilderness walks and game-viewing with professional guides are also available. Accommodation is provided in four lodges in the reserve.

Republic of Transkei

B3 10 Butterworth Founded in 1827, Butterworth is Transkei's oldest town and a major shopping and industrial centre. After making the necessary purchases, passengers laden with items as diverse as chickens, goats, furniture and bicycles are ferried back to the countryside on buses. The **Butterworth River Cascades** and the **Bawa Falls** close to the town are worth visiting.

C3 11 Coffee Bay Easy access from the N2 has detracted somewhat from the wildness of this resort. The beach is popular with surfers and the lagoon offers safe bathing. Cowries and other shells delight shell collectors; shad, blacktail and galjoen attract anglers.

C3 12 Dwesa Nature Reserve Large game such as rhino, buffalo and zebra as well as a diverse bird life may be seen here. The unspoilt coastline yields a rich variety of shells. Accommodation is available in bungalows close to the sea.

C3 13 Hole in the Wall This massive outcrop of rock rising from the sea is one of the well-known landmarks on Transkei's Wild Coast. The huge hole in the cliff has been eroded over the millenia by the pounding action of waves. Fishing in this area is excellent.

C3 14 Mazeppa Bay Shark fishing is one of the main attractions and large numbers of fishermen descend on the bay every August. Visitors will also enjoy the three beaches with prehistoric shell middens, giant sand dunes and rich oysterbeds. Trails lead from the bay past **Manubi Forest** with its yellowwood and sneezewood trees.

D2 15 Mkambati Nature Reserve Located between the Msikaba and Mtentu Rivers in an area noted for its rugged scenic beauty. The reserve has camping facilities and a single bungalow. A peninsula which is accessible only at low tide yields exotic cowries.

C2 16 Port St Johns Situated on the banks of the Umzimvubu River, the resort is a favourite retreat for those in search of a peaceful holiday. Excellent fishing, beautiful white sandy beaches and walks through the dense riverine forest may be enjoyed.

B3 17 Qolora Mouth The attractive subtropical coastal setting of the village and the long white beach make this a very popular seaside destination.

C2 18 Umtata The capital of Transkei exudes an old style charm with modern day amenities. The **Nduli Game Reserve** within the city limits is a peaceful refuge. Also of interest close to the city are the **Luchaba Nature Reserve** and the **Izandla Pottery School.**

B3, D2 19 Wild Coast Hiking Trail The trail of 280 km along one of South Africa's most dramatic coastlines is divided into five sections lasting from three to six days each. Overnight huts are available.

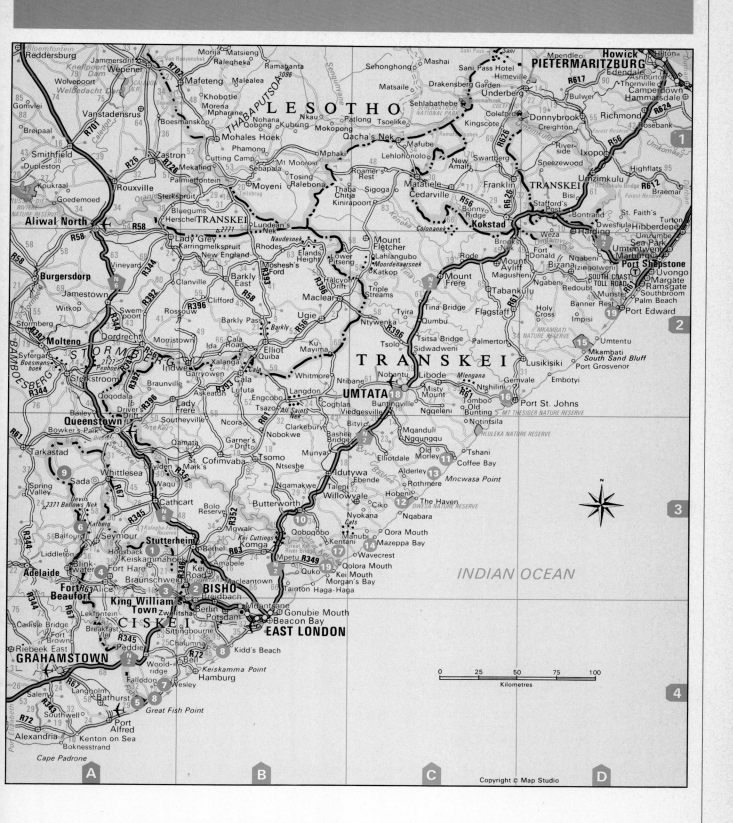

Northern Cape

The rugged regions of the northern Cape attract those who prefer to unwind at an easygoing tempo, those who relate to striking contrasts, broad horizons and silence. Bounded by Botswana in the north and the Orange Free State in the east, this vast area has only one city, one major town and a scattering of villages.

The Orange River surges across the landscape, at places in a sluggish tide, at others in powerful exuberance. The most dramatic point on the river occurs at the Augrabies Falls. The sight is breathtaking, the noise deafening, as the river plummets, roars and explodes in an awesome unleashing of power.

Upington, situated in an intensively cultivated agricultural area on the banks of the river, is the principal town of the northern Cape. Cotton, lucerne, wheat, grapes, sultanas and raisins are farmed here, as well as karakul sheep, goats and cattle.

Much of the area is occupied by the sandy Kalahari. From Upington to the Kalahari Gemsbok National Park, the road leads through undulating rust-red dunelands, marked haphazardly by crags, scattered grasses and clumps of camelthorn trees.

On the R27 between Upington and Vryburg, the town of Kuruman provides a pleasant stopover spot. The area is fresh and green, watered by the continual flow of the 'eye' (the source of the Kuruman River) which rises from a dolomite cave and yields 18 million litres of water a day, irrigating the district.

In 1866, an unusual 'pebble' was found near Kimberley on the banks of the Orange River. It was, in fact, a 21-carat diamond. Three years later, another stone was discovered in the same area. It weighed 83 carats. The discoveries precipitated the world's greatest diamond rush - and changed the course of history.

Top: Scattered bands of Bushmen inhabit parts of the semi-desert Kalahari region.

Above: Great herds of springbok roam the Kalahari Gemsbok National Park.

Top: The most dramatic point on the Orange River occurs at the Augrabies Falls.

Above: Fort outside Prieska, built by the British during the Anglo-Boer war.

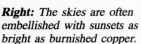

Right: The skies are often embellished with sunsets as bright as burnished copper.

Left: The lion is another easily identified inhabitant of the Kalahari Park.

110

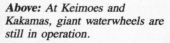

Above: *At Keimoes and Kakamas, giant waterwheels are still in operation.*

Right: *Upington, on the banks of the Orange, is the principal town of the northern Cape.*

Below: The gemsbok's sharp horns are excellent weapons, and respected even by lions.

Above: *Canoeists meet the challenge of the Orange River rapids.*

Left: *Twee Rivieren Rest Camp, at the Kalahari Park, offers comfortable accommodation.*

Below: *White sands and 'roaring' sands: an unusual feature of the little town of Witsand.*

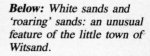

Places of Interest

A3 1 Augrabies Falls National Park

The waterfall is aptly described by the Hottentot name meaning 'place of great noise'. The park comprises a vast area of river landscape incorporating the impressive falls formed by the Orange River thundering 56 m into a granite gorge 20 m wide and 18 m long. Baboons, eland, springbok, other smaller antelope and black rhino inhabit the park. Accommodation is available in self-catering chalets and a caravan park. The three-day Klipspringer Hiking Trail leads through the reserve.

D3 2 Barkly West

Scene of the first diamond rush in the northern Cape in 1869. To this day the river diggings attract hopeful prospectors. At **Canteen Koppie** (Hill) there is an open-air archaeological museum and nature reserve. The **Mining Commissioner's Museum** in town houses many interesting exhibits.

E5 3 Colesberg

This Karoo town has retained much of its old-world ambience. A horse-driven mill and the quaint cottages in Bell Street, the British barracks with the last remaining horse trough, the museum in what was once the Colesberg Bank floated in 1861, the magistrate's office and the police station are reminders of the 19th century.

C4 4 Griquatown

The first mission station north of the Orange River was established here in 1803 and headed by Robert Moffat from 1820. The mission station and the original home of the family is now the **Mary Moffat Museum.**

A1 5 Kalahari Gemsbok National Park

The park constitutes one of the largest unspoilt ecosystems in the world. Despite the barren appearance, it is noted for its variety of game and birds, especially raptors. Accommodation is available in three rest camps.

B4 6 Kenhardt

Just south of the town on the main road to Cape Town is a forest of quiver trees (*Aloe dichotoma*). These strange succulent trees, also known as tree aloes, occur throughout the north-western Cape. Another conspicuous feature of the area are the very large, untidy nests of the sociable weaver found on telephone poles and trees. Fine examples can be seen on the gravel road to Kakamas.

C2 7 Kuruman

Of great interest here is the mission station established in 1826 by Robert Moffat, and the church which was the venue for the marriage of his daughter Mary to the explorer David Livingstone. Equally interesting is the source of the Kuruman River, known as the **'Eye of Kuruman'**. The fountain, regarded as one of the natural wonders of Southern Africa, yields some 18 million litres of water per day.

C3 8 Postmasburg

The town serves a mining district producing manganese, asbestos and diamonds. At **Gatkoppies,** five kilometres north-east of the town, archaeological findings indicated evidence of mining activity as long ago as 700 A.D.

C4 9 Prieska

Situated on the southern bank of the Orange River in an area noted for semi-precious stones. The **Prieska Koppie Nature Reserve** boasts an impressive collection of aloe and euphorbia as well as a stone fort dating from the Anglo-Boer War. The **Ria Huisamen Aloe Garden** also has a vast collection of succulents. Golfers playing on the local golf course will cross the Prieska River 18 times!

D3 10 Riverton

This holiday resort on the banks of the Vaal River offers accommodation and various recreational amenities. Water sports and bird-watching are favourite pastimes.

C3 11 Roaring Sands

An unusual natural phenomenon occurs at **Witsand** some 20 km south-west of Postmasburg. Any disturbance of the high dunes, particularly in hot dry weather, produces a weird moaning sound; hence the name. The dunes form part of the so-called white dunes, some 12 km long, which do not mix with the surrounding red sands that characterise these parts.

B3 12 Upington

Despite its location on the edge of the Kalahari Desert, Upington is surprisingly green - thanks to a system of canals from the Orange River. A holiday resort on **Olyvenhoutsdrif,** one of the many islands in the river, offers excellent facilities. Another resort on the northern banks of the river caters mainly for caravanners and campers. Other attractions include the **Kalahari-Oranje Museum,** the **Orange River Wine Cellars,** a dried fruit factory and the **Spitskop Nature Reserve** some 13 km north of the town.

D2 13 Vryburg

The district is often referred to as the 'Texas of South Africa' because of the extensive cattle-ranching. It is estimated that there are more than half a million head of cattle in the area. The **Vryburg Museum,** a pleasure resort close by and the adjacent **Taljaardt Nature Reserve** are worth visiting.

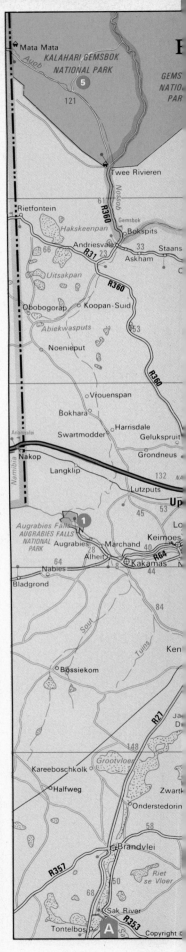

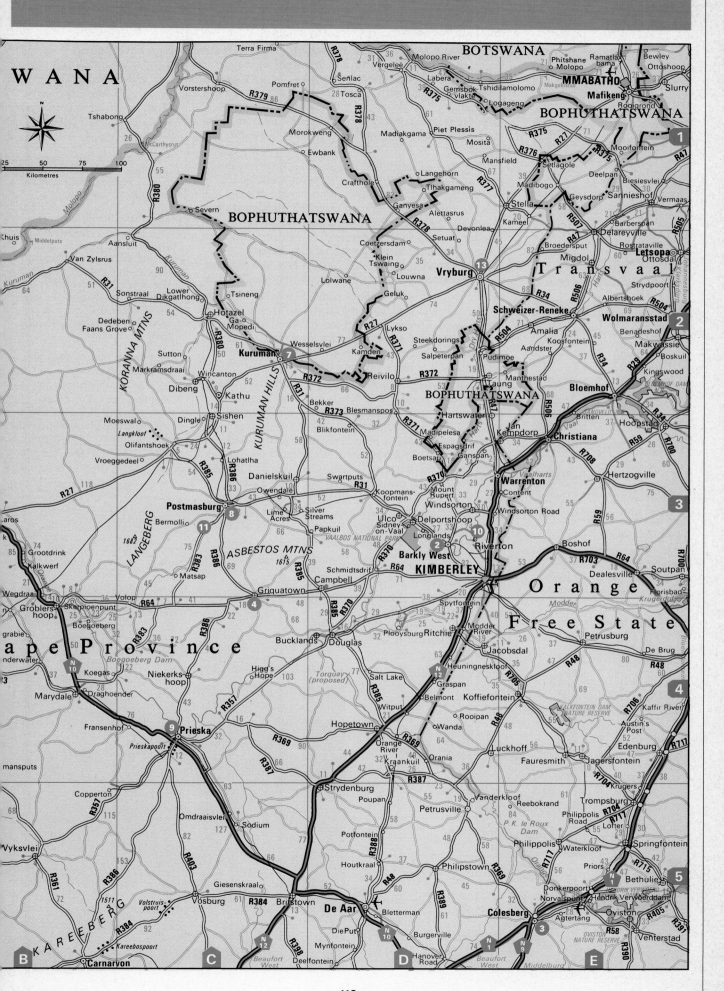

Kimberley

One of South Africa's most fascinating historical sagas began near Kimberley, with the discovery of the 21-carat 'Eureka' diamond in 1866 and the fabulous 83-carat 'Star of South Africa' in 1869. News travelled fast and, by the end of the 1860s, hordes of prospectors had converged on the region, scouring the river banks and sifting soil in a frenetic quest for wealth.

Kimberley was catapulted into an era of high stakes and ruthless power struggles. From an unlikely backdrop of heat, dust, flies and a jumble of tents and shacks, many ambitious men emerged from obscurity to achieve fame. Cecil John Rhodes, son of an English country vicar, became the wealthiest and most powerful man in the Africa of his day. Barney Barnato, who began life as a barrow boy in a London slum, became a mining magnate and multi-millionaire.

Before long, spacious homes began to rise from the dust; roads and bridges were built and, by the turn of the century, Kimberley had been transformed into a prosperous city - and South Africa was well on the way to establishing herself as the most highly industrialised country on the continent.

Today, Kimberley is a modern city with broad, tree-lined streets, comfortable hotels and busy shopping centres - far removed from the chaos of 130 years ago. But the extraordinary saga of its past seems ever-present, enveloping it in an aura of adventure and drama. If you close your eyes, it's easy to conjure up a picture of the diggers, loafers, gamblers and 'ladies' of ill repute who once inhabited the dusty shanty town.

Despite the fact that the mines are approaching the end of their lives, the name 'Kimberley' will always be synonymous with diamonds. In the words of former De Beers Chairman, Mr Harry Oppenheimer, 'the city will remain the capital of the world's diamond industry, even when all the mines around it are silent relics like the Big Hole'.

Top: 'Dunluce' — one of Kimberley's stately Victorian homes.

Above: Uncut diamonds are on display at the De Beers Hall, Kimberley Mine Museum.

Below: This statue of Rhodes portrays him as the people of Kimberley knew him best.

Suggested Tours

The following tours take place on a regular basis:

De Beers' Diamond Recovery Plant (conducted walking tour)

Taung Sun Hotel and Casino (Bophuthatswana)

Visitors with transport have the advantage of flexibility and a great many additional options, including the following:

The Diamond Route

Lies between Victoria West in the Cape and Potchefstroom in the Transvaal, passing through Hopetown, Kimberley and Warrenton. Notice boards giving information on places of interest en route have been erected at the entrance to each town.

Mmabatho Sun/Malopo Sun

(Bophuthatswana, some 250 km north of Kimberley.)

The Mmabatho Sun offers luxury and sparkling entertainment. Facilities include a small casino, sophisticated movies, video games, two pool

decks, and tennis and volleyball courts. Within a few minutes' drive, the Molopo Sun (no casino) has a swimming pool, an all-weather floodlit tennis court, snooker and an 18-hole putting course.

Augrabies Falls National Park (Approximately 120 km west of Upington, along the Orange River, passing Keimoes and Kakamas en route.)

Upington is a convenient overnight stop for visitors travelling to the Augrabies Falls National Park and the Kalahari Gemsbok National Park. Two hotels and a holiday resort provide comfortable accommodation.

The land around the much-photographed Augrabies Falls supports klipspringer, springbok, kudu and smaller mammals, some 52 species of reptiles and 180 bird species. The falls are the fifth largest in the world and prone to dramatic increases in their flow. According to legend, a fortune in diamonds lies at the bottom of the falls, washed down from sources far inland, but the sheer weight of water cascading down the cataract prevents investigation.

Kalahari Gemsbok National Park (The Twee Rivieren entrance is 320 km north of Upington.)

The semi-desert Kalahari is unlike any other park in South Africa. Variants of many species of fauna and flora have adapted to an almost waterless environment. The Nossob River flows perhaps once in 30 years, the Auob once in three.

Despite the shortage of rain, wildlife is surprisingly prolific and varied: leopard, cheetah and Kalahari lion; herds of springbok, gemsbok, eland and hartebeest. Animals trek in their thousands across the sandy plains. Between August and October, large herds gather in the river beds. Birds of prey include the bateleur and the martial, tawny and snake eagle.

Battlefields

Some of the Anglo-Boer War's most important battles were fought in the northern Cape: among them, the sieges by Boers of British garrisons at Kimberley and Mafeking (now part of Bophuthatswana). During the battle of Magersfontein, 30 km from Kimberley, the British force was defeated and the Highland Brigade almost annihilated. An observation post overlooks the battlefield and trenches. A museum houses a collection of war relics, and a relief map with troop and gun positions depicts the battle. This was one of the three battles of 'British Black Week', fought in 1899 during the first phase of the war.

For further information on tours and details of tour operators, restaurants, shopping centres, specialist shops and accommodation, contact your nearest SATOUR office (see back cover) or the Kimberley Publicity Office (see page 121).

Above: The 'Big Hole' is all that remains of the Kimberley Mine. About 14.5 million carats of diamonds were excavated from its depths.

Right: Ladies brought a few social refinements to the rough and rollicking shanty town of the early days.

Below: Trams were introduced in 1887. Today, a historic tram runs between the City Hall and the Mine Museum Village.

Left: The Diggers' Fountain commemorates the contribution made by the thousands of diggers who toiled on the mines.

Places of Interest

B3 1 Africana Library The collection of northern Cape Africana includes the missionary Robert Moffat's original translation of the Bible into Tswana and the printing press on which he printed the work.

B3 2 Alexander McGregor Memorial Museum Displays depict southern Africa's natural history, geology and prehistory.

B5 3 B J Vorster Airport Situated some six kilometres outside the city. There are no buses from the airport to town but major car hire firms are based at the airport.

C3 4 Belgravia Kimberley's oldest exclusively residential suburb features many beautiful homes which date from 1873 to the present.

D5 5 Bultfontein Mine This mine five kilometres out of town is still operational and surface tours of the treatment and recovery plants are offered twice a day from Tuesdays to Fridays. Advance booking is required for underground tours.

B2 6 City Hall An imposing building in the classic Roman Corinthian style. Kimberley was the first city in Africa to illuminate its streets by electric light. Replicas of these original lights now grace the exterior of the city hall. The Kimberley Information Office is situated at the city hall.

C4 7 Duggan-Cronin Gallery Incorporates a unique collection of photographs of the indigenous people of southern Africa taken between 1919 and 1939 by Alfred Duggan-Cronin, a turn-of-the-century De Beers night-watchman. Displays include historical background to the Black people of South Africa.

C4 8 Dunluce Built in 1897, Dunluce with its long verandahs and ornate decorations is one of Kimberley's most stately homes and an outstanding example of late Victorian domestic architecture. The mansion forms part of the McGregor Museum. Guided tours are offered by appointment at the museum.

C4 9 Halfway House Hotel Drive-in Pub South Africa's first drive-in pub is believed to be one of only two in the world (the other being the pub at the Kimberlite Hotel, also in Kimberley). In Rhodes' day men imbibed here on horseback. Today customers may order a drink without leaving their cars.

B4 10 Honoured Dead Memorial Designed by Sir Herbert Baker on the lines of a Greek tomb in Sicily, the memorial commemorates those who died during the Siege of Kimberley in 1899. The 28-lb gun 'Long Cecil' which was produced within 24 days during the siege, is on display.

A3 11 Kimberley Mine Museum and Big Hole This open-air museum depicts Kimberley in its Victorian heyday during the greatest diamond rush in history. It incorporates a group of buildings dating from those heady days. They include a church, diggers' tavern complete with honky tonk piano, Barney Barnato's Boxing Academy, the De Beers directors' private railway coach, shops, houses and other relics of the early mining days. An observation platform offers a good view of the **Big Hole,** all that remains of the former Colesberg Koppie (hill) where diamonds were discovered early in 1870. The hole has a circumference of 4,572 m, a diameter of 1.5 km and an area of 11 ha. During the 43 years that the area was mined (1871-1914) some 25,000,000 tons of blue ground were removed from the mine yielding 2,722 kg of diamonds.

C4 12 McGregor Museum Housed in a gracious building erected in 1897 as a sanatorium. Exhibits reflect the environment of the northern Cape, the early history and development of Kimberley, and the most opulent period in the history of the city.

B5 13 Pioneers of Aviation Museum Situated three and a half kilometres beyond the airport at Alexandersfontein on the road to the Danie Theron Combat School. The museum on the site of South Africa's first flying school which was established in 1913 features a reconstruction of the original hanger and a replica of the Compton-Paterson biplane used in flight training. The flying school was the forerunner to the establishment of the South African Air Force. An exhibition of photographs depicts the history of the Air Force.

C3 14 Rudd House This gracious house built in 1888 was the home of the mining magnate H P Rudd whose father was a great friend and business partner of Rhodes. It has been restored as a period house in the opulent style of the mega-magnates. Guided tours are available by appointment at the McGregor Museum.

C3 15 Sister Henrietta Stockdale Chapel Sister Henrietta Stockdale was an Anglican nun and the first matron of Kimberley Hospital. Her efforts to secure legal recognition for the nursing profession led to South Africa instituting compulsory registration of nurses in 1891 - the first country in the world to do so. The chapel built in her honour can be visited by contacting the nurses' home.

A2 16 Star of the West Pub Established in 1870, this pub was a popular haunt of the diggers. It is believed to be the oldest continuously functioning bar in South Africa. Mementoes of the past include Rhodes' custom-made barstool.

C5 17 Tram service Kimberley is so steeped in history that the refurbished vintage tram which transports passengers from the city hall to the Mine Museum does not seem at all out of place. Tickets are sold on the tram. Special trips may be arranged at the Kimberley Information Office at the city hall.

A2 18 William Humphreys Art Museum A fine collection of South African paintings, as well as masterpieces of the Dutch, Flemish, English and French Schools are on display.

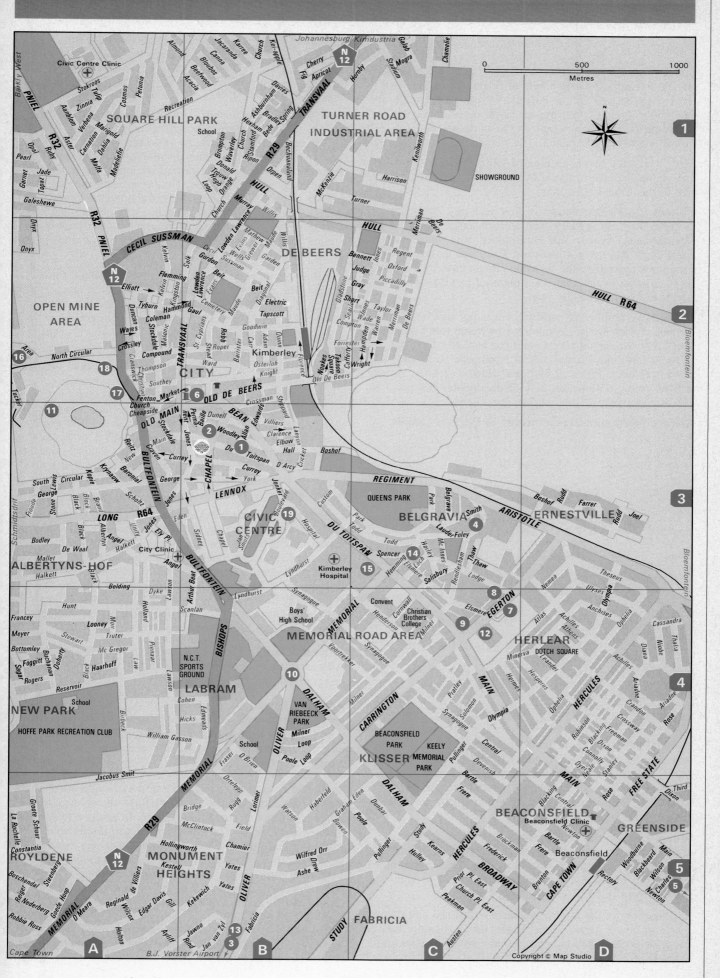

Fast Facts

Location and Boundaries At the southernmost tip of the African continent, the Republic of South Africa (RSA) is flanked in the west by the Atlantic Ocean, in the south and east by the Indian Ocean, in the north by Namibia, Botswana and Zimbabwe, and in the north-east by Mozambique and Swaziland.

Size The RSA covers an area of 1,127,200 sq km - about one eighth the size of the USA, and nearly five times the size of the United Kingdom.

Climate Midwinter occurs in June and July, midsummer in December and January. The climate ranges from Mediterranean in the Cape Peninsula to subtropical on the Natal coast and the north-eastern Transvaal; temperate conditions prevail on the highveld. In general, a perennially sunny climate means that it's a pleasure to visit South Africa at any time of the year.

The average number of sunshine hours per day is 8.5, compared with 3.8 in London, 6.4 in Rome and 6.9 in New York. The average hours of sunshine annually for Cape Town (2,980) and Pretoria (3,240) compare favourably with London (1,480), Rome (2,360) and Hawaii (2,450). Annual rainfall averages 464 mm; 21% of the country has less than 200 mm per year.

Average Maximum Temperatures in Degrees Celsius

Cape Town	26.5	27.1	25.8	23.0	19.9	18.5	17.2	18.1	19.1	21.5	24.0	25.5
Pretoria	28.8	28.1	26.8	25.1	22.5	20.2	19.1	22.7	25.7	28.3	28.1	28.7
Johannesburg	26.3	25.6	24.3	22.1	19.1	16.5	16.4	19.8	22.8	25.0	25.3	26.1
Port Elizabeth	25.4	25.5	24.6	22.8	21.9	20.1	19.5	19.9	20.1	20.9	22.4	24.0
East London	25.2	25.6	24.7	23.5	22.6	20.9	21.0	21.3	21.4	21.6	22.8	24.0
Durban	27.2	27.5	26.9	25.6	24.1	22.5	22.0	22.4	22.9	23.6	24.9	26.2
Bloemfontein	29.8	28.3	26.3	22.8	19.0	16.6	16.4	19.6	22.8	25.8	27.5	29.2
Kimberley	32.5	31.0	28.4	25.3	21.2	18.6	18.5	21.8	24.6	28.3	29.9	31.7
Nelspruit	29.1	29.0	28.2	26.8	25.1	23.1	23.3	24.9	26.7	27.2	27.6	28.5

Physical Features Sun, wind, rain, rivers and the opposing influences of two currents, one cold, the other warm, have given rise to a phenomenal spectrum of awe-inspiring landscapes: mountains, plains, plateaux and coastlands, lakes and lagoons, deserts and sun-scorched 'moonscapes'.

Provinces, Capitals and Major Cities The country is divided into four provinces: the Cape Province, Transvaal, Orange Free State and Natal. There are three capital cities: Cape Town (legislative), Pretoria (administrative) and Bloemfontein (judicial).

Johannesburg is the largest industrial, financial and cultural centre in South Africa. Cape Town and Durban are two of the most popular holiday playgrounds. Notable cities and towns from a historical and cultural point of view include Pietermaritzburg, Grahamstown, Graaff-Reinet, Port Elizabeth, Kimberley and Stellenbosch.

Population The population is currently estimated at approximately 35,000,000.

Most Whites are descended from Dutch, French, British and German immigrants who settled in the country between the 17th and 19th centuries. In more recent times, the country has attracted additional immigrants from these countries, as well as other parts of Europe, China and Africa north of the Limpopo. Unofficial estimates put the number of people of Portuguese extraction (the largest group of recent immigrants) at half a million. It's said that apart from New York, there is no city outside Israel which is quite as Jewish as Johannesburg, where some 60% of the country's 120,000 Jews live.

The Black population is made up of several major ethnic groups. The majority are Zulus, followed by Xhosas, North Sothos, South Sothos, Tswanas, Shangaan-Tsongas and Swazis. All are descendants of tribes who migrated south from central Africa. About 50% of South Africa's Blacks are urbanised.

The majority of Coloureds (people of mixed racial origins) inhabit the western Cape. Cape Malays, a subgroup, number about 200,000, and most inhabit the Cape Peninsula, with a heavy concentration in Cape Town's Malay Quarter. The first Asians arrived in 1860 to work on Natal's sugar-cane fields, and today over 85% of South Africa's Indians live in Natal. After India, Pakistan and Sri Lanka, South Africa's Indian community is the fourth largest in the world. Many are prosperous merchants, traders and professional people.

Languages English and Afrikaans, the official languages, are spoken throughout the country. Official notices and road signs appear in both languages. Each of the Black groups has its own language. Urbanised Blacks are usually competent in English and/or Afrikaans. A number of (mainly older generation) Indians still speak the languages of their forefathers, but the practice is gradually falling away in favour of English. Languages such as French, German and Italian are spoken by staff members at many up-market hotels and shops.

Infrastructure Efficiency is the keynote of the South African infrastructure: travel and accommodation reservations may be relied upon with confidence.

Access The national carrier, South African Airways, and several international air and shipping lines link the country with the rest of the world. South Africa's international airports are situated in the vicinity of Johannesburg, Durban and Cape Town.

Domestic Transport Road and transport systems are the finest on the continent. The road network links all centres, from the largest metropolis to the tiniest village. In addition to domestic airlines, the following transport options are available: railways (the Blue Train offers a five-star ride), inter-city coaches and fly-drive safaris. 'Designer' tours, arranged to suit individual preferences, are offered by a number of tour operators. Major international car hire companies are represented in South Africa.

Accommodation Standards are generally high. All tourist accommodation establishments belonging to the national grading and classification scheme are graded and classified. A one-star

118

grading ranks as good; five stars indicate that the establishment is outstanding. Classification indicates those establishments that offer superior standards of service and hospitality.

In addition to hotels, tourist accommodation encompasses motels, holiday flats and chalets, beach cottages, game lodges, guest farms and youth hostels. Caravan/camping parks occur throughout the country. Time-share units are a relatively new, but fast developing concept.

On a limited scale, accommodation in private homes provides an attractive option. Farm holidays are catching on fast, and these are offered throughout the country - a boon for city people who yearn for wide open spaces and a simple life style.

Communication A direct dialling service connects all local centres except for tiny villages in remote country districts. Europe, North and South America, Australia, New Zealand and India, the Republic of China, Hong Kong, Japan and Israel are among a large number of places where subscribers may be dialled direct. Major hotels and businesses have telex and fax services.

Electricity Most city and town power systems are 220/230 volts AC at 50 cycles per second. The Pretoria power system generates 250 volts and Port Elizabeth 220/250 volts. (Adaptors for electric shavers and hair driers are obtainable locally.)

Water Tap water is purified and 100% safe to drink.

Malaria/Bilharzia Precautions Visitors to the eastern Transvaal lowveld and northern Natal should take anti-malaria tablets before, during and after their stay. Obtainable without prescription from local pharmacies. It is inadvisable to swim in rivers and lakes in the eastern and northern regions of the country, as the bilharzia parasite may be present in the water.

Monetary System The South African currency unit is the Rand, denoted by the symbol R. R1 = 100 cents.

The Rand Exchange Rate is in Your Favour! In addition to shopping bargains, an up-market hotel will cost you a fraction of the tariff charged by equivalent establishments elsewhere. And the same applies to fine cuisine and wine, entertainment and transport.

VAT (Value Added Tax) VAT, currently at 14%, is included in the marked/quoted price of most goods and services. Foreign tourists may claim refunds of VAT paid on goods which they take out of South Africa. Information leaflets on the procedure to follow to claim VAT refunds are available from Vat Refund Administration offices at the Beit Bridge Border Post, Jan Smuts Airport (Johannesburg), Louis Botha Airport (Durban) and DF Malan Airport (Cape Town). Queries should be directed to: VAT Refund Administrators, 106 Diamond Exchange Building, 85 De Villiers Street, Johannesburg; PO Box 9478, Johannesburg, 2000; telephone (011) 29 6441. The leaflets are also available from Satour offices.

Touring South Africa

Day 1:
Early morning arrival at Jan Smuts Airport. Hire a car at the airport and transfer to your hotel in Johannesburg (N1) or Pretoria (N1) [approximately 35 km].

JOHANNESBURG
Among a great many other attractions, you can visit Gold Reef City (open-air museum) and enjoy the spirit of the great gold rush era. Features include a Victorian fun fair, old brewery, public house and stock exchange. Watch a gold pour and enjoy traditional tribal dancing; underground, you can explore the workings of a gold mine.
For further information, see pages 18 - 21.

OR

PRETORIA
A tour of the administrative capital of South Africa should include the Voortrekker Monument, a view of the city from the Union Buildings, the National Zoological Gardens (ranked among the world's 10 best) and Melrose House.
For further information, see pages 22 - 25.

Day 2:
Johannesburg/Pretoria (N4) - Middelburg - Waterval Boven - Schagen - Sudwala - Nelspruit/White River. [Johannesburg - White River = approximately 380 km; Pretoria - White River = approximately 360 km.]

From Johannesburg/Pretoria, travel either via the Premier Diamond Mine near Cullinan where the largest diamond ever found in South Africa (3,025 carats) was mined, or drive direct via Middelburg and Waterval Boven to Schagen. En route to Sabie, visit the Sudwala Caves and the adjacent Dinosaur Park which contains life-sized replicas of prehistoric mammals and reptiles.

Day 3:
Nelspruit - White River (R40) - (R537) Mac-Mac Falls - Graskop - Pinnacle Rock - God's Window - Berlin - Lisbon Falls - Pilgrim's Rest - Blyderivierspoort. [Nelspruit - Graskop = approximately 150 km; Pilgrim's Rest - Blyderivierspoort = approximately 70 km.]

Drive via the peaceful forestry town of Sabie, set in an enormous man-made forest, to Mac-Mac Falls. Continue to Graskop for a view of Pinnacle Rock, and onward to God's Window which offers panoramas of the lowveld 1,000 m below. Follow a small detour past the Berlin and Lisbon Falls, and return to Graskop. Continue to Pilgrim's Rest, a living museum and perfect replica of a 19th century gold rush town.

Day 4:
Pilgrim's Rest - (R533) - Bourke's Luck Potholes - (R36) - Blyderivierspoort - Abel Erasmus Pass (R531) - Klaserie - Orpen - Satara [approximately 260 km].

OR

Blyderivierspoort (R527) - (R40) - (R530) - Phalaborwa - Letaba - Olifants Rest Camp [approximately 250 km].

The Bourke's Luck Potholes at the confluence of the Blyde and Treur Rivers consist of deep cylindrical cavities formed by the swirling action of pebble-laden flood waters. Continue to the Blyderivierspoort Nature Reserve and the Blyde River Canyon - an immense ravine carved out of the face of the Drakensberg Mountains. Then travel via the Abel Erasmus Pass to the subtropical lowveld town of Hoedspruit.

For further information, see pages 34 - 37.

From Hoedspruit, drive via Mica to Phalaborwa and the world famous Kruger National Park. It's advisable to keep your cameras handy after you enter the park.

OR

About 13 km before Hoedspruit, turn right (R531) and continue south towards Klaserie. Just after Klaserie, follow the road in the direction of the Orpen Gate to the Kruger National Park. This is the largest wildlife sanctuary in the Republic of South Africa. Internationally renowned, it supports the greatest variety of wildlife species on the African continent: 137 mammal species, 493 bird species and 112 reptile species.

For further information, see pages 10 - 11.

Advance booking for weekends and public and school holidays is essential.

Day 5:

Olifants/Satara Rest Camps - Skukuza - Berg-en-Dal/Lower Sabie Rest Camps (Kruger Park).
[Olifants - Berg-en-Dal/Lower Sabie = approximately 200 km.]

Olifants/Satara: Savour the dawn, tune in to birdsong and the awakening of the animal world. At Skukuza, you can visit an interesting museum and enjoy lunch in an old railway carriage. Your game drive through the southern section of the park to Lower Sabie/Berg-en-Dal Rest Camps promises to be full of surprises.

Day 6:

After an early game drive, travel via Nelspruit back to Johannesburg.

OR

Kruger National Park (R38) - Barberton - Badplaas (R33) - Amsterdam - Piet Retief (R29) - Pongola (N2) - Mkuzi/Hluhluwe Game Reserves.
[Lower Sabie - Mkuzi Game Reserve = approximately 600 km.]

Early morning game drive before leaving Kruger Park. Travel via Kaapmuiden and Barberton (old mining town) to Badplaas; continue via Lochiel and Amsterdam to Piet Retief. The journey to Mkuzi/Hluhluwe Game Reserves leads through the rolling hills of Zululand, dotted with traditional beehive huts.

Day 7:

At leisure in Mkuzi/Hluhluwe.

Mkuzi is characterised by low-lying thornveld, attractive trees and a diverse and plentiful wildlife. Some 413 bird species have been recorded here. You have the option of self-drive game viewing excursions or guided walks and wilderness trails. There are four hides where game may be observed and photographed at close range.

Hluhluwe encompasses a combination of forest, woodland and grassland, and supports a great diversity of wildlife, including the black and white rhino. Birds are numerous and varied; crocs and hippos occur in the rivers. Boat trips on the Hluhluwe River may be arranged.

For further information, see pages 10 - 11.

Day 8:

Mkuzi/Hluhluwe (N2) - Empangeni (R34) - Shakaland - Nkwalini (R68) - Eshowe - Gingindlovu (N2) - Umhlanga Rocks/Durban.
[Mkuzi - Umhlanga Rocks = approximately 380 km.]

After an early morning game drive and breakfast, you drive through parts of Zululand (KwaZulu), the traditional home of the Zulus - the largest black group in South Africa. Over three million Zulus live here under the leadership of Chief Mangosuthu Buthelezi - one of South Africa's best known and most respected politicians.

At Empangeni, turn onto the R34 in the direction of Eshowe and visit the traditional Zulu kraal, 'Shakaland', where you can have lunch and learn something about the history and culture of the Zulu people. Continue to Gingindlovu or Mtunzini along the Natal north coast to the popular beach resort of Umhlanga Rocks, some 19 km north of Durban. Year round bathing on the Natal coast.

For further information, see pages 52 - 55.

Days 9, 10 and 11:

At leisure in Umhlanga Rocks/Durban.

Up-market Umhlanga has something for everyone: broad, sandy beaches, exclusive shopping centres, excellent hotels and a sophisticated nightlife. En route to Durban, shoppers will be tempted to browse around the excellent La Lucia Shopping Mall, open seven days a week.

For further information, see pages 40 - 43.

Day 12:

Umhlanga Rocks/Durban (N3) - Pietermaritzburg - Mooi River - Estcourt (R74) - Winterton - Bergville - Royal Natal National Park/Cathedral Peak/Cathkin Peak [approximately 310 km].

En route to the Drakensberg, make a point of spending a few hours in historical Pietermaritzburg. From there, travel to Howick via the R103 in the direction of Nottingham Road. Continue via Estcourt and Winterton to the South African 'Alps' - the Drakensberg.

For further information, see pages 44 - 51.

Day 13:

At leisure in the Drakensberg.

Day 14:

Drakensberg hotel - Harrismith (N3) - Warden - Villiers - Heidelberg - Johannesburg [360 - 410 km].

OR

Day 12:

Umhlanga Rocks/Durban (N2) - Park Rynie (R612) - Ixopo (R56) - Umzimkulu (Transkei border) (N2) - Kokstad - Umtata (R61) - Port St Johns.
[Umhlanga Rocks - Umtata = approximately 460 km; Umhlanga Rocks - Port St Johns = approximately 560 km.]

Transkei visas are issued at the border post.

For further information, see pages 56 - 59, 108 - 109.

Day 13:

Port St Johns (R61) - Umtata (N2) - Idutywa - Butterworth - Kei Cuttings (Transkei border) - Bisho (R63) - Fort Hare - Hogsback.

For further information, see pages 108 - 109.

Day 14:

Hogsback (R345) - (R63) - Fort Beaufort (R67) - Grahamstown (N2) - Port Elizabeth [approximately 270 km].

For further information, see pages 96 - 103.

Travellers can return their hired cars in Port Elizabeth and fly back to Johannesburg.

O R

Day 15:

Port Elizabeth (N2) - Tsitsikamma Forest - Plettenberg Bay - Knysna [approximately 290 km].

For further information, see pages 92 - 95.

Day 16:

Knysna (N2) - George (N12) - Oudtshoorn (R328) - Mossel Bay
[Knysna - Oudtshoorn = approximately 120 km;
Knysna - Oudtshoorn via Mossel Bay = approximately 190 km.]

The Garden Route is one of the great scenic attractions of the country. There are dozens of seaside resorts and tranquil villages where you can stop for refreshments. A number of magnificent passes over the mountains lead to the Little Karoo. Oudtshoorn, the major centre of the Little Karoo, is also known as the 'Feather Capital of the World' because of the large ostrich industry in the area. Two show farms, 'Highgate' and 'Safari', are open daily. A highlight for some visitors is a ride on an ostrich. Ostrich delicacies feature on the lunch menu.

For further information, see pages 92 - 95.

Day 17:

Oudtshoorn (N2) - Swellendam (R319) - Bredasdorp - Cape Agulhas (R316) - Waenhuiskrans (Arniston) - Hermanus.
[Oudtshoorn - Cape Agulhas - Arniston = approximately 400 km;
Oudtshoorn - Cape Agulhas - Elim - Gans Bay - Hermanus = approximately 470 km.]

From Cape Agulhas - the southernmost point of Africa - drive to Waenhuiskrans (also known as Arniston) via Elim and Gans Bay, or to Hermanus - a scenic resort on the shores of Walker Bay.

Day 18:

Waenhuiskrans (Arniston) (R316) - Bredasdorp - Caledon - Die Vlei - Franschhoek - Stellenbosch.
[Waenhuiskrans - Caledon - Elgin - Franschhoek - Stellenbosch = approximately 190 km.]

OR

Hermanus - Franschhoek - Stellenbosch.
[Hermanus - Botrivier - Elgin - Vyeboom - Theewaterskloof Dam - Franschhoek - Stellenbosch = approximately 130 km.]

Fifty percent of South Africa's apple exports are produced in the Elgin region. The Franschhoek/Paarl/Stellenbosch area is the most important wine-growing region in the country. The Cape Wine Routes lead through a countryside adorned with mountains, forests, vineyards and old gabled homesteads. Most wine estates offer cellar tours and tastings; some have restaurants. While in wine country, you should make time to explore the towns after which the routes are named.

For further information, see pages 84 - 87.

Day 19:

Stellenbosch (M12) - Bellville (M13) - Bloubergstrand (M14) - (M6) - Sea Point - Clifton - Hout Bay - Chapman's Peak Drive (M65) - Kommetjie - Cape Point Nature Reserve (M4) - Fish Hoek - Muizenberg - Kirstenbosch Botanical Gardens (Cape Town) [approximately 230 km].

Bloubergstrand is famous for its breathtaking view of Table Mountain and Cape Town. The Cape of Good Hope Nature Reserve conserves Cape flora (including the King protea which is the national flower of South Africa), and wildlife such as eland, bontebok, black wildebeest, rhebok, grysbok, springbok and baboon.

For further information, see pages 76 - 79, 84 - 87.

Days 20 and 21:

At leisure in Cape Town.

For further information, see pages 80 - 83.

Publicity/Marketing Associations

Your travel agent should have all the additional information you require. Most South African cities and towns have publicity associations which offer pamphlets, maps, information and advice.

Major South African Publicity/Marketing Associations and Telephone Numbers:

Bloemfontein Publicity Association (051) 405 8490

CAPTOUR (Cape Tourism Authority) (021) 418 5214

Eastern Province Tourism Association (041) 55 8922

George Publicity Association (0441) 74 4000

Graaff-Reinet Publicity Association (0491) 2 2479

Grahamstown Publicity Association (0461) 2 3241

Greater Durban Marketing Authority (031) 304 4934/ 304 4981

Greater East London Publicity Association (0431) 2 6015

Johannesburg Publicity Association (011) 29 4961

Kimberley Tourist Information (0531) 80 6264

Knysna Publicity Association (0445) 2 1610

Lowveld & Escarpment Tourist Paradise (01311) 59 2270/1

Margate Publicity Association (03931) 2 2322

Mossel Bay Publicity Association (0444) 4526

Nelspruit Publicity Association (01311) 59 2033

Noordtratoer (Northern Transvaal) (01521) 95 2011

Northern Cape Tourism Association (0531) 80 6264/5

Pietermaritzburg Publicity Association (0331) 45 1348/9

Plettenburg Bay Business and Publicity Association (04457) 3 4066

Port Elizabeth Publicity Association (041) 52 1315/6

Pretoria Information Bureau (012) 313 7410

Stellenbosch Publicity Association (02231) 9 9633

TANK (Tourism Association of Natal and KwaZulu) (031) 307 7494

Western Cape Tourism Association (021) 913 2336